THE RISE AND FALL OF THE
KU KLUX KLAN
IN NEW JERSEY

D1568498

THE RISE AND FALL OF THE
KU KLUX KLAN
IN NEW JERSEY

JOSEPH G. BILBY AND HARRY ZIEGLER

THE
History
PRESS

Published by The History Press
Charleston, SC
www.historypress.com

First published 2019

Manufactured in the United States

ISBN 9781467142625

Library of Congress Control Number: 2019940044

This book is dedicated to the citizens of New Jersey who witnessed the rise of the Ku Klux Klan, saw it for what it was and defeated it.

CONTENTS

ACKNOWLEDGEMENTS

I t is impossible to research and write on the 1920s Ku Klux Klan in New Jersey without consulting the massive collection of documents, newspaper clippings and other sources gathered on the subject by Bernard Bush, which are now preserved in Rutgers University's Alexander Library. Without the Bush collection, this would have been a far more laborious project. In addition, invaluable information and images were provided by the George H. Moss Jr. Historical Collection of Stereo Views and Ephemera; Guggenheim Memorial Library; Monmouth University in West Long Branch, New Jersey; the collections of the New Jersey Historical Society in Newark; the InfoAge Museum archives in the former Klan headquarters at the Marconi site in Wall Township; the Monmouth County Clerk's Office; the Newark Library; and the New Jersey Historical Society.

We also wish to thank the following individuals for their valuable assistance, suggestions, critiques and encouragement, without which this project could not have been accomplished: James Amemasor, Adam Azzolino, Ted Bell, John Bilby, Bernard Bush, Fred Carl, Joyce Helen Fredman, Randall Gabrielan, Joseph Grabas, Tom Irving, Fred Packman, Bob Perricelli, George Severini, Steven Tettamanti, Frank Tomasello, Gregory Urwin, Kurt Wagner, John Zinn and Melissa Kozlowski Ziobro. If we have inadvertently missed anyone, please accept our apologies.

Note from Dorn's Classic Images on Image Usage
Dorn's makes its Klan photos available only to historians and educators. They are not for sale to the public because Dorn's firmly condemns the philosophy and activities of the Ku Klux Klan.

INTRODUCTION

I n retrospect, it all seems unlikely. How could an itinerant huckster like William J. Simmons revive a secret society dedicated to the return of the social, economic and political status quo of the Confederacy, sans legal race-based human slavery, nearly a half century after it was suppressed and then sell it as a patriotic fraternal order to people in every state in the nation? It was, as are many things in history, complicated.

The times were unfortunately troubled and anxious. In an inauspicious coincidence, a revolution was simultaneously taking place in entertainment, which played a consequential role in this story. Simmons was a salesman, and his product was membership in numerous fraternal organizations, providing a sense of emotional security and belonging that had originated in the nineteenth century. In a society where many people felt increasingly alienated, Simmons's pitch was reassuring enough to blind people to the potential malignancy of the actual agenda.

The massive publicity gained by the 1915 breakthrough film *The Birth of a Nation*, which reinforced and spread inaccurate history of the Reconstruction period, turned a distorted southern myth into a national one and dovetailed with the "reconciliation movement" and the monument-raising campaign of the United Daughters of the Confederacy, which was intended to obscure the actual cause of the Civil War.

Adding to the general apprehension and uneasiness of the era was the impact of a new wave of immigrants, most of whom did not speak English or share the same religious beliefs as most native-born Americans. Increased labor activism came to the fore as well and, in many cases, was supported by foreign-born radicals. The public disillusionment of the times was intensified by the histrionic jingoism and xenophobia created during World War I, when government agencies launched a massive propaganda campaign and spied on the public. Prohibition became icing on the anxiety cake, magnifying all sorts of social and cultural changes.

In New Jersey, although many white Protestants regarded Catholics, Jews and immigrants with wariness and circumspection, these new New Jerseyans, along with a growing African American community, represented a large proportion of the state's population. This demographic spread would make it difficult for the Klan to gain a secure and lasting foothold in the state.

New Jersey Klan leader and salesman Arthur H. Bell and his wife, Leah, two of the key players in the rise and fall of the Klan, were former vaudevillians and used Klan events as public theater to advertise and recruit for the organization. They were also in the habit of exaggerating the actual membership of the New Jersey Klan—a practice shared by the national organization.

In New Jersey there was (thankfully) no Klan-related violent vigilantism, lynching or collusion with political or law enforcement personnel, although intimidation was often used as a tool. In the years since its final legal dissolution in 1946, the New Jersey Ku Klux Klan has barely been mentioned. During the civil rights era, some racists in hoods engineering the occasional cross burning against African Americans, even in New Jersey, created an illusion that there was a defined and unbroken lineage between the perpetrators of those incidents and the historical second iteration of the Klan, but this was not the case.

The following pages detail the unlikely rise of the New Jersey Klan, the self-generated hyperbole that surrounded it, the reaction it inspired and, ultimately, the organization's rapid downfall. Every state's experience with the Klan differed, of course, and New Jersey's was unique in a way only New Jersey could be.

CHAPTER 1

"A MAN CHRONICALLY ON THE MAKE."

t made film history and played at theaters across the nation for years. It was the "photo-play" known as *The Birth of a Nation*. A pioneering film released in 1915, it provided national credence to the fabricated "lost cause" concept of the Civil War—a faux-history fantasy in which noble Confederates fought for independence and were victimized after the conflict by thieving Yankee "carpetbaggers" who callously moved in to plunder them. According to this narrative, carpetbaggers manipulated gullible freed slaves—eager to avenge themselves on their former masters—into assisting them in the creation of a reign of terror. Then came the Ku Klux Klan.

Audiences were understandably impressed by producer/director D.W. Griffith's massive battle scenes in an artform that was previously limited to minimal action with few actors on small, even cramped, sets. Most newspaper reviews of Griffith's epic stressed his depiction of the rise of the Klan as an organization that saved southern womanhood and preserved social order, portraying that as the most significant segment of the film.

New Jersey papers were no exception. Across the state, the coverage was laudatory. The *Trenton Times* noted:

> *The Ku Klux Klan, which forms such an interesting part of D.W. Griffith's great production "The Birth of a Nation," was organized as a secret and social band in the State of Tennessee in May, 1866....In subsequent years when the Klan went forth to put down the desperadoes who swarmed down from the North to grab everything in sight in the South, the riders adopted the emblem of the fiery cross which the Scotch Highlanders had long used as a call to battle.*

D.W. Griffith, director of the film *The Birth of a Nation*, which inspired the rebirth of the Ku Klux Klan. *From Library of Congress.*

In 1916, the *New Brunswick Home News* wrote, "The great deeds of the Civil War and the horrors of Reconstruction are made to live again and the nation reborn is apotheosized."

In 1918, the *Bridgewater Courier News* concluded, "From the first scene to the last the film maintains the keenest interest, but it reaches its strongest point in the second part, when the hordes of the Ku Klux Klan are gathering for the rescue of harried whites."[1]

One of many inspired by the film, especially its portrayal of the Ku Klux Klan, was thirty-five-year-old William Joseph Simmons. Simmons, described by one historian as "a man chronically on the make," who could be classified as a middle-class ne'er-do-well, had a varied career. The Alabama-born Simmons was a medical school dropout who had served several months as a private in the First Alabama Infantry in the Spanish-American War and was a failed employee of the Methodist Church. In his most successful effort, as a salesman of memberships in fraternal societies (he was allegedly a member of fifteen), Simmons portrayed himself as a doctor and a minister and promoted himself to "colonel" based on his rank in the Woodmen of the World organization.[2]

In 1915, while recovering from an auto accident in Atlanta, Simmons apparently saw *The Birth of a Nation* and, realizing there was money to be made, decided to revive the Ku Klux Klan. Although he offered a dubious alternate explanation—that he had "visions" of resurrecting the Klan since childhood—the date of the resurrection suggests that *The Birth of a Nation* was the catalyst. Simmons claimed that he consulted an instruction manual from the original Klan to organize his updated version of the order and, with some of his friends and a few elderly men who were allegedly veterans of its first iteration, literally reignited the organization by burning a cross atop Stone Mountain, Georgia, on Thanksgiving night in 1915.[3]

Given to the aggrandizing harangues that would become a trademark of the revived Klan, Simmons maintained that he had heroically raised the cross in "a temperature far below freezing," although, in fact, it was around forty-five degrees Fahrenheit that evening. The burning cross was a dramatic

Left: An advertisement for a showing of *The Birth of a Nation*, which spread a false view of the Reconstruction era across the nation, making heroes out of the Ku Klux Klansmen of the post–Civil War era. *From Joseph Bilby*.

Right: Actress Lillian Gish, the heroine of *The Birth of a Nation*, portrays a noble southern woman being leered at by, in this case, a Union soldier. *From Library of Congress*.

image borrowed from the film, which in its turn lifted it from the novel the movie was based on, *The Clansman* by Thomas Dixon Jr. Dixon claimed Scottish clan members brought the practice to the United States South.

Fraternal orders of all types appealed to late nineteenth-century American middle- and working-class men. The groups helped in-need members' families in the absence of a government safety net and affordable life insurance. They also provided men with participatory entertainment, a sense of community in an urbanizing society as well as a sense of belonging to something bigger than themselves, which they believed beneficial not only to local interests but to the country at large. Added to that was the benefit of networking for jobs and other economic advantages. Ceremonial claptrap, strange titles, secret passwords and bizarre attire added to the aura of intrigue and exclusivity, connoting a sense of importance to groups of otherwise ordinary men. One survey of Ku Klux Klan members in a county in Michigan in the mid-1920s revealed that 73 percent of them also

William Joseph Simmons, "a man constantly on the make," who created the second Ku Klux Klan in 1915. *From Library of Congress.*

belonged to other fraternal organizations. As an experienced fraternal order huckster, Simmons was aware of this appeal and, tellingly, advertised his new Klan as a "Classy Order of the Highest Class."[4]

With characteristic grandiosity, Simmons dubbed himself the "Imperial Wizard of the Invisible Empire of the Knights of the Ku Klux Klan." His organization did indeed remain invisible outside the immediate Atlanta region for several years, garnering only a few hundred members at best, although a membership list was never disclosed. Looking to boost adherents, Klansmen claimed they were in patriotic pursuit of World War I draft dodgers, but the only public appearance of the new Klan was at a veterans' parade in 1919. At one point, ironically, since the Klan later became a major defender of prohibition, Simmons allegedly proposed a private "bottle club," exempt from the provisions of the Volstead Act, as a recruiting enticement.[5]

A turnaround occurred when Simmons hired marketing professionals Edward Young Clarke and Elizabeth Tyler of the Southern Publicity Association (providers of public relations to the Anti-Saloon League, among

Actual KKK members circa 1869. Although they did don masks, the white robes and peaked hoods of the second Ku Klux Klan are mostly theatrical inventions of D.W. Griffith. *From Library of Congress.*

other organizations), who promised they could turn his mediocre local fraternity into a national organization. The duo wrote speeches for Simmons, polishing his presentation and expanding his rhetoric beyond complaints of black people's racial "heredity handicap." Under their guidance, Simmons expanded his target list to immigrants, Jews, Catholics, labor agitators, "Bolsheviks" and political radicals of any stripe, along with the cultural aspects of the Jazz Age. Clarke and Tyler launched a public relations blitz of press releases and advertisements and arranged newspaper interviews with Simmons. The Imperial Wizard agreed to pay the couple a sizable portion of the financial returns from an expanded Klan. Clarke later recalled that the necessity of demonizing Catholics and Jews would cost him friends, so he wanted to ensure a good payoff in return.[6]

Such complaints against "outsiders" were nothing new. Clarke, Tyler and Simmons were exploiting a long-standing trait of frightened people—resorting to prejudice. This tendency was exacerbated by the still-prevalent rationalizations for race-based slavery and periodic anti-immigrant outbursts in American society. Racial anxiety had peaked once more in the South in the wake of World War I, as black men returned from Europe, where many had fought, albeit under French command, against the Germans in 1918. These veterans were ready to claim their full rights as citizens, and their protests led to a record number of lynchings—some with soldiers still in uniform—across the South. Perhaps the ultimate result of this paranoia was the horrible race riot of 1921 in Tulsa, Oklahoma. The wealthiest African American neighborhood in the country was ravaged by a white mob, and three hundred people were killed. Klansmen were allegedly involved as members of law enforcement and National Guard units charged with keeping the peace.[7]

As a bonus, the Clarke/Tyler message was delivered to a public used to the government-sponsored, hyper-patriotic fervor and xenophobia of World War I and its aftermath, as fear of immigrant radicals grew following the Bolshevik Revolution. A bomb exploded on Wall Street in front of the J.P. Morgan Bank in September 1920, killing thirty people and injuring more than one hundred more. Although the case was never solved, the perpetrators are thought to have been Italian anarchists. In the wake of the incident, Attorney General A. Mitchell Palmer rounded up Communists, anarchists and those suspected of any sort of radical tendency, deporting many under dubious legal premises in 1919 and 1920. The new Ku Klux Klan, composed of white Protestants, offered itself as the only solution for the dangers to the United States.

The expanding Klan suffered a public relations setback in a 1921 *New York World* exposé of the order's vigilante violence, dubious monetary practices and tax avoidance. The paper added a little spice to the story by reporting that Clarke and Tyler had been arrested while partially clothed in a "disorderly house." The result was a congressional hearing where "Colonel" Simmons, in his role as pseudo-archetypal southern gentleman, denied the charges. Simmons insisted that his organization did not advocate violence and that its fiscal policies were the same as any other fraternal organization. In the end, no serious investigations were launched, as congressmen wanted to stay out of an allegedly patriotic organization's business.[8]

The New York City pro-immigrant, left-wing weekly newspaper *Issues of Today*, which was dedicated to "Social Decency and Civic Justice," praised the *World's* investigation, calling it "one of the finest achievements in American journalism" and recommending it as "the sort of thing our papers can and should do." Unfortunately, the result was not, as many had hoped, the downfall of the Klan.[9]

Despite temporary embarrassment, Clarke and Tyler turned the publicity from the incident into a recruiting opportunity. The *World* series ironically created nationwide interest in the organization, and newspapers and magazines across the country increased their own Klan coverage as a result. Even though most of the publicity was negative, it succeeded in drawing recruits to the order. What was profitable to the media proved profitable to the Klan as well.[10]

Clarke and Tyler capitalized on the new notoriety by reaching out to fraternal societies and Protestant churches, offering free membership to ministers. Recruiters, known as "Kleagles," spread out across the country to uncover which fears made different communities anxious. They tested African American equality, Jewish and Catholic subversion, speakeasies and bootleggers, sexual licentiousness and local political corruption, among other real and/or imagined social ills. All were present in a time of tumultuous cultural change and became convenient excuses to rouse the population. The diversity of the Klan's enemy list could cover almost anything a self-appointed "100 percent American" was concerned about in the 1920s. The Klan also offered its members the opportunity to serve as reformist enforcers, which were similar to the World War I Bureau of Investigation vigilantes who spied and reported on "slackers" avoiding the draft, German sympathizers, anti-war civilians and taverns serving soldiers. In 1921, the Klan, boasting more than 100,000 members nationwide, began to establish state "Realms," which oversaw local "Klaverns."[11]

The recruiting and expansion proved very profitable to the Klan leadership. Probably the most important aspect of Clarke and Tyler's operation was the creation of a pyramid-type recruiting scheme in which Kleagles offered memberships for a $10 "Klectoken," or initiation coin, from which the Kleagle would get $4, the state "King Kleagle" in charge of Realm Recruiting got $1, the Grand Goblin of the Realm got $0.50, Clarke and Tyler got $2.50 and Simmons got $2.

There were other channels of profit as well. The Klan was formally incorporated and engaged in a contract for "official" garb with an Atlanta garment manufacturer and another with a publishing company, allegedly run by Clarke, to print the organization's manuals and publications. Clarke also founded a real estate company that charged a fee to manage the Klan's growing property holdings. The couple reportedly earned $850,000 (approximately $12 million in today's money) in the initial fifteen months of their campaign.[12]

By the summer of 1920, rumors of an expanding Klan had reached New Jersey from Pennsylvania. In August, a *Trenton Times* report noted that "a masked band of night riders, wearing white helmets and astride white caparisoned horses," galloped through McConnellsville. Mounted policemen attempted to follow them but lost the trail. The paper went on to note, "Citizens who saw the horsemen prophesied another Ku Klux Klan movement, while others declared that the costumes worn by the riders were the same as the Mormons wore in their early colonization days in the west." There is little doubt, however, that the riders, whether they were Klansmen or pranksters, modeled their garb on the Klan as portrayed in *The Birth of a Nation*.[13]

In March 1920, New Jersey governor Edward I. Edwards, a dedicated foe of prohibition who had promised to keep the state "as wet as the Atlantic Ocean," apparently referring to the post–Civil War organization, compared the Anti-Saloon League to a "latter day Ku Klux Klan." By the end of the year, a New Jersey newspaper was commenting rather ominously on a Klan march with two hundred participants in South Jacksonville, Florida. The paper reported that the marchers were "completely disguised in white caps, masks and gowns and headed by a herald bearing a flaming cross. No explanation of the display was given."[14]

In the summer of 1921, Clarke, now the Klan's "Imperial Kleagle," sent his recruiters into New Jersey, where the organization was initially viewed as a curiosity. The *Trenton Times* printed a Clarke/Tyler press release as a news story, identifying "Colonel Joseph Simmons, now professor of southern history in Lanter [sic] University, Atlanta, Georgia," as the leader of the Klan. The article went on to provide the Klan's definition of its purpose as:

> *To inculcate the sacred principals [sic] and noble ideas of chivalry, the development of character, the protection of the home and the chastity of womanhood, the exemplification of a pure and practical patriotism towards our glorious country, the preservation of American ideals and institutions and the maintenance of white supremacy.*[15]

The *Trenton Times* article also informed the public that the new Klan organizing secretly in the cities "has been especially successful in Newark and Elizabeth" and had plans of opening a Trenton headquarters "soon." That intent evoked a rapid response from African American war veterans of the American Legion's Mitchell Davis Post. In a letter to Mayor Frederick W. Donnelly, the members of the post declared that they would oppose any attempts to establish a Klan chapter in Trenton, as it would be "regrettable" since "there is at present no feeling between races such as the Ku Klux Klan might incite."

New Jersey governor Edward I. Edwards was a dedicated foe of prohibition and promised to keep New Jersey "as wet as the Atlantic Ocean." *From Joseph Bilby.*

Trenton Commissioner of Public Safety George P. Labarre was more forthright. He told a journalist, "If the [Klan] members do commit any acts tending to race war or such disturbances, they may as well know that they will be sent to jail or shot down in cold blood, if necessary."

In a calmer vein, an African American Republican politician from Hudson County, George Cannon, saw little need to be alarmed. Cannon thought the Klan a primarily southern organization and believed it "would not be likely to gain much strength in New Jersey."

Dean William Pickens, field secretary of the NAACP, disagreed and argued a necessity for "undivided cooperation with the Catholic Church and all other agencies through which the terrible and un-American attempts of the Ku Klux Klan may and can be completely frustrated."[16]

In Plainfield, the Shiloh Baptist Church held a sunrise prayer meeting in September 1921. The church's African American parishioners were "deeply concerned about the Ku Klux Klan movement…and they believe that the time has arrived when they should take prompt and effectual means to defeat the purpose of the [KKK] propaganda."

There was no Klan activity in Plainfield at the time, and city officials assured citizens that "such an organization would not receive any encouragement in Plainfield, believing it to be a dangerous movement, and one that does not tend for the betterment of the community."[17]

It is puzzling that the Klan, with its broadened mission of opposition to Catholics, Jews and immigrants, thought its best recruiting opportunities were in the cities of a state in which, according to the 1920 census, 20 percent of the population was foreign-born and, in the beginnings of the Great Migration, was 5 percent African American. Most of the people the organization opposed lived in those cities where they were recruiting. Perhaps Clarke thought the remaining "real Americans" in New Jersey's urban areas would be properly horrified by the influx of "others" and be easy pickings.[18]

Demographics would become more unfavorable to the New Jersey Ku Klux Klan as the years went by. One survey of the population published in 1942 reported:

The state ranks fifth in the country in its percentage of foreign born. The 1930 census showed that New Jersey's population was divided as follows: 57% were either foreign born or had one or both parents born abroad; 5% were Negroes; and 38% were native whites of native parentage. These native whites were chiefly of English, Scotch, Dutch or Irish origin. The foreign nations from which the largest numbers of immigrants have come to New Jersey in the last fifty years are Italy, Germany and Poland.

The survey added, "There is a larger proportion of Jewish people in New Jersey than in any other state, except New York." It should be noted that most of the native-born people of Irish heritage were Catholic.[19]

Whatever Clarke's reasoning, his recruiters came to Paterson, Newark and Elizabeth. Kleagles Orville Cheatham and Russell F. Trimble established a headquarters at 837 Broad Street in Newark (the building now houses a nail salon), and Cheatham showed journalists maps and charts that he alleged represented active Klan chapters all over the state.

Cheatham extended an invitation to Newark mayor Alexander Archibald to join the Klan. The mayor brusquely rejected it. Archibald told the press that "Newark is a pretty well governed city and can take care of itself without the assistance of the Ku Klux Klan." Public Safety director William F. Brennan added that if the Klan was composed of "100 percent Americans," why did they "go around wearing masks"? The Newark chapter initiated its first recruits on September 20, 1921, and in

New Jersey was home to a large number of immigrants, and in 1920, the number of foreign-born residents of the state was 20 percent of the population. That number included this Hungarian family from Elizabeth, New Jersey, seen here in a twentieth-century cabinet photo. *From Joseph Bilby.*

late 1922, Cheatham formally established George Washington Klavern No. 3 in the city, which eventually claimed to have two thousand members. The actual number is unknown, as there are no surviving records, and the Klan was—to be kind—given to exaggeration.[20]

Arguments opposing the Klan expansion into the state varied. An *Asbury Park Press* editorial from September 1921 reinforced the *Birth of a Nation* myth that the organization was indeed necessary during Reconstruction because "the slave had been freed and carpet-baggers had swarmed through the land utilizing the Negro ballot thru playing on the ignorance of the freed slaves." The editorial went on with a conclusion that those "peculiar conditions" did not justify a revival of the Klan by "race antagonizers" and "could not be cited as a justification for the organization of the Ku Klux Klan." The *Press* concluded that "the present Ku Klux Klan has no place in a democracy."[21]

On August 30, 1921, a decidedly hostile *Newark Evening News* editorial opined that the Klan "was not welcome here" and declared that the organization was a "negation of democracy, an autocratic group of self-appointed reformers who try to take the kingdom of heaven by violence, a futile effort that was exploded some 2,000 years ago." The *News* went on to claim that "masks are to conceal. They are badges of cowardice, of lawlessness, of motives not shared by the majority of citizens."[22]

On September 14, the *Asbury Park Press* published a major article about attempts to establish Ku Klux Klan chapters at the New Jersey shore, particularly Asbury Park. The paper cited secret recruiters' standard initial approaches to Protestant ministers, who received literature portraying the Klan as a virtuous and patriotic fraternal order. The article revealed that "the gist of the information contained in one pamphlet is to the effect that the Klan is supposed to be a certifiable incarnation of patriotism and lofty purpose." The pamphlet was accompanied by a form with twenty questions for a potential candidate, including whether his parents were born in the United States and whether he was "a gentile or a Jew" or "white or colored."[23]

An additional piece of literature in the packet used a quote from President Woodrow Wilson's book, *A History of the American People*. Wilson was born in the South but became president of Princeton University and then New Jersey governor. He declared that "adventurers swarmed out of the north as much the enemies of one race as the other to cozen, beguile and use the Negroes....The white men were roused by a mere instinct of self-preservation—until, at last, there had sprung into existence a great Ku Klux Klan, a veritable empire of the south, to protect the southern land." Wilson, at a private showing of *The Birth of a Nation* in the White House, allegedly declared it "true history."[24]

The *Asbury Park Press* article concluded that the course the recruiting effort would take was speculative but that it had "gotten the whole shore section talking about the merits and disadvantages of membership in the Klan." Though not disputing the lost-cause myth about the original Klansmen as saviors who "returned home rule" to the South, the story also noted that in other states, hooded Klansmen from the revived order had taken the law into their own hands to settle private grudges. Despite the paper's reservations, the Jersey shore counties of Ocean and Monmouth would become Klan strongholds within a few years.[25]

By the end of 1921, the Ku Klux Klan had established itself in New Jersey as a bizarre, hyper-secret club with sealed membership lists, and the people of the state would, in succeeding years, be alternately enraged and entertained by the group's antics. This was not because early opposition waned—anti-Klan fervor actually increased throughout the 1920s.

CHAPTER 2

"TAR AND FEATHERS FOR YOU."

F ollowing the tumult of the final months of 1921, when the revived Ku Klux Klan announced its arrival in New Jersey and gained a response that was, to say the least, less than enthusiastic, things quieted down. Kleagles went about their work in secret, organizing and making recruiting pitches to ministers and fraternal organizations around the state, while Klan members periodically attempted attention-grabbing stunts, hoping to make the news.

In May 1922, five robed and hooded Klansmen carrying two American flags and a wooden cross appeared at the Third Presbyterian Church in Elizabeth, much to the surprise of the congregation, which was singing "Onward, Christian Soldiers." The visitors marched down the center aisle to the pulpit and handed an envelope to the pastor, Reverend Robert Mark, then turned and left. Mark proceeded to preach a sermon in which he defended Klan activities as a counter to the Knights of Columbus, who, according to him, sent money to Ireland to fund attacks on Protestant church services in Belfast.[26]

The envelope contained a twenty-five-dollar donation and a note that read, in part:

> *The Elizabeth Klan takes great interest in watching the activities of the churches of our city and we therefore feel that the enclosed donation will show our sincere approval and appreciation of the administration of your*

Third Presbyterian Church and Parsonage
Elizabeth, N. J.

Central Baptist Church

The Third Presbyterian Church in Elizabeth, New Jersey, where Klansmen carrying two American flags and a wooden cross made a theatrical donation in May 1922. *From Joseph Bilby.*

deacons' fund. The Ku Klux Klan stands firmly on the following principles: White supremacy, protection of women and sanctity of the home, separation of church and state, pure Americanism.

Reverend Mark said he had no idea that the visit would occur, although that is unlikely, considering these church donation performances were well-known Klan tactics and "Onward, Christian Soldiers" had become a kind of Klan anthem.

In June, the *Asbury Park Press* announced that the Klan had "been working quietly" in that city to recruit members. Information in the article was provided by Klansmen, who advised that "four hundred members…met in an unknown part of this city…and initiated new members." It was reported that "a local merchant had been scheduled to be initiated and give a speech but owing to his alien birth discovered at the last minute, he could not join the order."[27]

A journalist following up on the story reported that "many local men have been approached to join. Many have acquiesced, and many have turned down the order." He confronted real estate agent Alfred D. Fourett, who had an office on the third floor of the Appleby Building on Mattison Avenue and was reputed to be the local Kleagle. Fourett admitted that he had encouraged men to join the Klan but denied that he was a Kleagle or even a member of the organization. He did highly praise the Klan for being "100 percent American" and a supporter of "good government." Fourett said he had no idea where the alleged mass meeting had taken place and did not know who the local Klan leader was. The idea that four hundred Klansmen could meet in a small city like Asbury Park without anyone noticing strains credulity and should be taken with, perhaps, more than the proverbial grain of salt.[28]

The Klan even made a bold move in Paterson, a likely uphill battleground, since the "silk city" was a hotbed of radical labor activists and anarchists with a large immigrant population. Although no members appeared or identified themselves in public, the "Paterson Klan No. 15, Knights of the Ku Klux Klan, Invisible Empire, Realm of New Jersey," wrote to Mayor Frank J. Van Noort to protest the mayor's decision to close the city's schools so children could attend the funeral of Father William McNulty, pastor of Saint John's Catholic Church. The mayor was honoring the request of an ecumenical group of ministers, priests and rabbis in showing respect for the popular priest. The correspondence from the Klan claimed that "this organization wishes to go on record as being opposed to the closing of our public schools for any sectarian purpose." Van Noort ignored the request, ordered flags around the city flown at half-mast and issued a statement that read, "For threescore years Dean McNulty has been a force in the community for law and order and better citizenship."[29]

The Paterson Klavern, which later named itself "Leif Erikson Klan No. 1," was described as the first "major unit" of the Klan established in New Jersey. It seemed to manifest its existence primarily by writing letters to public officials rather than appearing in public, which makes one suspect its actual membership was small. On another occasion, the Paterson chapter, evoking World War I propaganda, protested the restoration of German language instruction in the city schools and described the United States' problems as rooted in "German-Bolshevist-pacifist-radical-internationalist propaganda."[30]

There was a more positive response to the Klan in smaller communities, especially those transitioning from rural to suburban areas and experiencing an influx of Catholic and Jewish immigrants. Such

School closings for the funeral of Father William McNulty, pastor of Saint John's Catholic Church in Paterson, were protested by the Klan. *From Joseph Bilby*.

was the Bergen County town of Hillsdale, where the local Klan leaders, Alpheus and Albert Rawson, privileged sons of a scamster father with a strong sense of theater, had progressed from juvenile, quasi-criminal pranksters to vigilantes under the protection of the Bergen County Detectives Association. This organization later evolved into the New Jersey Rangers Detective Association. Originally intended to protect Bergen County residents from "hobos" migrating from New York City and New Jersey urban centers, the group was a natural fit with the paranoid amateur law enforcers pursuing draft evaders and supposed German sympathizers during World War I. There is no evidence that any of these organizations led to an increase in the safety of local residents, but they were a manifestation of the social fears of the era that gave rise to the Klan. The Rawsons were prime examples of the type of self-important local opportunists attracted to the organization.[31]

While the Klan marched on, if unsteadily, in New Jersey, there were significant changes at the Atlanta headquarters. Founder William Joseph Simmons, despite the puritanical social ideals professed by the order, liked horse racing, boxing and consuming alcoholic beverages. His habits did not sit well with Hiram Evans, a pudgy Alabama-born dentist and Klan leader from Texas, who plotted with Edward Clarke and Elizabeth Tyler to con the con man. They convinced Simmons to accept a newly created faux position of "Emperor for Life," while Evans assumed the title of Imperial Wizard—the actual leader of the Klan—in November 1922. While the takeover could be viewed as a coup, Simmons was not entirely on the short end. He had to be bought out as Klan corporate CEO for $140,000 (more than $2 million in 2016).[32]

Evans saw himself as a reformer of sorts and immediately fired his co-conspirators, Clarke and Tyler, although they retained control of the Klan property management company in the Atlanta area. (This was a crew, for all their professed idealism, that always had a backup plan.) The new Imperial Wizard had grand ideas to dramatically expand the Klan's political influence and, with that in mind, moved his personal office from Atlanta to Washington, D.C., although Klan corporate headquarters remained in Atlanta. He also put recruiters on salary rather than commission and urged them to investigate the backgrounds of potential recruits more thoroughly. But, as with his predecessor, Evans's main aim was to expand the Klan nationally.[33]

Despite the turmoil in Atlanta, New Jersey King Kleagle George W. Apgar was no doubt satisfied with his stealth offensive. Recruiting, according to his Kleagles, was going well in the state. On September 8, 1922, Apgar, who was proprietor of a business that made artificial limbs, walked out of his home at 527 Washington Street in Hoboken to his car, which required physically turning a crank to start the engine. As happened occasionally, the crank kicked back on Apgar—which was bad enough—and then the car lurched forward and ran over the Kleagle, seriously injuring him. He was hospitalized at North Hudson Hospital in critical condition, creating an opening for a new King Kleagle.[34]

Several men succeeded Apgar, but the most notable one would prove to be Arthur Hornbui Bell. How Bell ascended to the position is, due to the secrecy of the Klan and lack of surviving records, unknown. What is known is that Bell was born in New York in 1891, and he and his wife, Leah, were vaudevillians who combined a song and dance act with ventriloquism. During World War I, the duo served overseas as YMCA entertainers for the army. Although several historians have maintained that Bell was an attorney,

Imperial Wizard Hiram Wesley Evans, the Texas dentist who succeeded the ousted William J. Simmons. *From Library of Congress.*

Left: Arthur and Leah Bell as YMCA entertainers in World War I. *From Wikimedia Commons.*

Below: A Klan initiation ceremony. The sponsoring Klansmen are robed while the initiates, known as "aliens," await their induction. The encircling automobiles can be seen in the background. This ceremony took place in central New Jersey, though the specific location is unknown. It may be the October 1922 ceremony Arthur Bell invited journalists and photographers to observe. *From the Collections of the New Jersey Historical Society, All Rights Reserved.*

there is no evidence for that claim. His census entries record that he left high school after his sophomore year and consistently gave his occupation as either "entertainer" or "salesman."

With Bell's influence in recruiting, the Klan became more visible—and theatrical—in New Jersey. In October 1922, in an abandoned quarry between Bernardsville and Summit, he staged a public "naturalization," Klan speak for initiation ceremony, of two hundred candidates from nine New Jersey cities. Reporters and photographers were advised that while they could not actually attend the ceremony, they would be able to observe it from the rim of the quarry.[35]

One newspaper reported that, in addition to the inductees, the event was attended by "about 800 Klansmen, half of them garbed in the white robe and hood of the order." It is not likely that Klansmen would attend such an event unrobed, and those not in costume were most likely relatives or friends, but Bell succeeded in creating a media impression that the Klan was large and growing. In an interview after the event, the new King Kleagle brought up his organization's self-declared police auxiliary role, stating that "the Klan had been working tirelessly to bring to justice the murderer of Reverend Edward Wheeler Hall and Mrs. James Mills of New Brunswick."[36]

Bell's reference was to a recent notorious murder case. On September 22, 1922, Reverend Edward Wheeler Hall, an Episcopal priest in New Brunswick, was found dead from gunshot wounds, along with his mistress, Eleanor Reinhardt Mills, a member of the church choir, in De Russey's Lane in Franklin Township, New Jersey. Suspicion fell on Reverend Hall's wife, Frances, and her brothers, but they were not arrested nor indicted at the time. The crime became popularly known as the "Hall-Mills Murders." Needless to say, the Klan played no part in the investigation, save in the publicity generated by Arthur Bell.

Continued newspaper speculation on the Hall-Mills Murders led Governor A. Harry Moore to request a new inquiry into the case in 1926. The investigation led to indictments of Frances Hall and her brothers for murder and a trial that began on November 3 and lasted thirty days. Although the accused had the motive and ability to commit the murders, the evidence to convict them—especially the erratic testimony of the witness, a farmer on whose property the bodies were found, "pig woman" Jane Gibson—was not convincing to the jury, and they were acquitted.

The case became national news and the biggest New Jersey crime story in history until the Lindbergh kidnapping. Oddly enough, in his 1964 book *The Minister and the Choir Singer*, later reprinted as *The Hall-Mills Murder Case*,

Site of the murder of Reverend Edward Wheeler Hall and his mistress, Eleanor Reinhardt Mills, in De Russey's Lane in Franklin Township, New Jersey. *From Joseph Bilby*.

radical activist attorney William Kunstler concluded that the Ku Klux Klan was responsible for the murders. He used a rather scattershot labyrinthine analysis with examples from other states to imply a political reluctance to criticize or investigate Klan vigilantism that never existed in New Jersey. In the end, he "conceded that the case against the Klan is entirely a circumstantial one" but still maintained it was a possibility. It wasn't.[37]

Another example of the Klan's expanded public relations campaign was the "discovery" of a letter regarding an initiation ceremony in December 1922, in Newark, where the George Washington chapter, then located at 17 West Park Street (today's Prudential Drive), would finally receive its charter. One Klansman told a reporter that the Klavern would initiate "between fifty and seventy-five new members" and hear an undisclosed "message of world-wide importance" conveyed from the Atlanta headquarters. The message was probably regarding the ascension of Hiram Evans to the Imperial Wizard title. The spokesman went on to claim that the Washington Klavern of Newark now had "a membership of one thousand five hundred, with four hundred more waiting to be initiated."[38]

The actual story is somewhat different. A *New York Times* reporter arrived at the address, a five-story brick building where the Klan rented a hall on the top floor, and encountered "half-a-dozen unmasked men, apparently awaiting induction, and a masked man who asked his business." When the reporter identified himself, the hooded Klansman left and returned with another, who said he was a Kleagle, and denied that the organization "was opposed to Catholics, Jews or Negroes, or was in any way un-American."[39]

More alleged initiates, a total of around thirty, straggled in as the reporter interviewed the Kleagle. In closing, the *New York Times* man was advised that "the Klan would soon turn out in hoods and gowns in Newark." Detectives Sweeney and O'Gorman of the Newark Police Department stood nearby, looking unimpressed.[40]

There would be one more Klan appearance in Newark before the end of the year. On December 22, 1922, the patients at the Newark Hospital for Crippled Children were having their Christmas party when a spooky, hooded Santa showed up. The staff requested that he remove his garb so as not to scare the children. He did and then presented a donation of fifty dollars to the hospital in the name of the Klan.[41]

As the New Jersey Ku Klux Klan slipped out of the closet in 1922, it apparently became a vehicle for pranksters and others determined to harass real or imagined enemies of its name. One case occurred in December in the Glendola section of Wall Township. Local farmer Oliver Youmans was the subject of printed placards that were "nailed to various telephone poles" around the town instructing him to "respect your mother" or be subjected to "tar and feathers for you." The warnings "bore the signature 'III K No Prints,'" which was taken as an implication of Ku Klux Klan involvement. A newspaper report doubted that conclusion, though, since "as far as anyone in Glendola seems to know, the Ku Klux Klan never has been in existence in that locality." The conclusion of local authorities was that someone "availed themselves of the Klan's reputation to attain their own ends." Ironically, by the middle of the decade, the New Jersey realm of the Ku Klux Klan's state headquarters would be sited in the Glendola section of Wall Township and would be a factor in the beginning of its end.[42]

CHAPTER 3

"MY GOD. DON'T DO THAT. IT'S MURDER."

The year 1923 began with a lull in New Jersey Ku Klux Klan activity. In February, a survey of newspaper editors around the state concluded, "Membership in the Ku Klux Klan in New Jersey is quite widespread, but comparatively inactive." To provide a perspective on the Klan's significance in New Jersey at this point in time, the feedback from the editors and cities is shown below in its entirety.

Newark *Star Eagle*: "We have not had any stories of the Ku Klux Klan here in a year, except one about three months ago. There is an organization here but judge it does not amount to much in membership."

Jersey City *Jersey Journal:* "The Ku Klux Klan is not extensive in Jersey City. We have never heard of it out in the open."

Paterson *News*: "The activities of the Klan here are confined to giving donations to charitable institutions. Money was presented to the Florence Crittenton Home at Eighteenth Street and Sixteenth Avenue and to the First Baptist Church, the Rev. Frank McDonald, pastor. I think there are prominent people connected with the Klan here, although their activities have not been in the open."

Elizabeth *Times*: "The Ku Klux Klan here is very quiet. Nearly a year ago it gave a church [Third Presbyterian] $25. It has disappeared from public view since then. Donald Bate, who was organizer in this section of the state, left and went to Florida after he had been thrown out of the order by W.A. Clarke, King Kleagle, at Atlanta."

Weehawken *Hudson Dispatch*: "The Klan, if it is here at all is very small. We have never been able to find it."

Passaic *Daily News*: "No demonstrations here. We know of no activities."

Trenton *State Gazette*: "There are no evidences of the Ku Klux Klan here."

Long Branch *Record*: "There is at present time no active organization. I say that from my own actual positive knowledge. Over a year ago a Klan was organized with about 50 members. Apparently, it was never completed. Within the last two or three months other organizers have come here, but so far as I have learned, without success. I know there is a Klan at Asbury Park, however, in good running condition."

Perth Amboy *Evening News*: "I never saw any trace of it here."

New Brunswick *Home News*: "If it exists here it is so quiet that it is not worth considering. We have had no evidence of it whatever in a year."

Camden *Courier*: "About a year ago an organizer came here and formed a branch of the Ku Klux Klan. He got about 100 members. The organization fell flat, however, after it had been pounded pretty hard for three or four months. The organizer went over to Philadelphia and was driven out of that city. The Klan seems to have disappeared from Camden County."

Atlantic City *Gazette Review*: "It has been said that a Klan exists here. But we can find no indication of it. Certain threatening letters received on KKK stationary were really written on letterheads that had been cut off, apparently above a previous letter, and were probably not written by authentic Ku Klux Klan members at all."

Bayonne *Evening News*: "There are evidences that the Ku Klux has a fair-sized organization here. A certain doctor is believed to be its examining physician, and another man well known about the town is supposed to be its organizer. The newspapers have received letters from certain persons attacking others for their criticism of the Klan."

Asbury Park Press: "The Ku Klux Klan has never shown any public signs of activity here, altho it is believed several local people are members of it."

Hackensack *Record*: "It has been reported that a Klan exists here, but we have never been able to locate anyone who will admit it, except one man who was not a regular resident of Hackensack, and he has since moved away. It is understood that about a year ago 15 Hackensack men were initiated at East Paterson. But they have shown no signs of activity since then."[43]

IN FEBRUARY 1923, THE Klan made another appearance in Newark. The city's Washington Park was the site of an eight-and-a-half-foot-tall statue of George Washington. The figure, by sculptor John Massey Rhind, was a portrayal of the general at the time of his farewell address to the Continental army at Rocky Hill, near Princeton, on November 2, 1783. On Washington's Birthday, Klansmen made a furtive midnight visit to the statue and laid a wreath with a note that it had been placed by the Klan. The police chief had the wreath removed the following morning.

Subsequently, "three men in heavy overcoats and slouch hats" who refused to give their names appeared at the offices of the *Newark News* and presented a reporter with a letter claiming it

> *was a sad homily upon conditions in Newark, and one which is receiving serious attention in Protestant circles when a wreath bearing American flags and placed on the statue of General Washington as a memorial to an American citizen by a body of Protestant all-American Gentiles is confiscated at the behest of a police chief for no other reason than that it was placed there by Protestant Gentiles....Warning is hereby given that this matter is going to be threshed [sic] out with all the virility at our command.*

There is no evidence, however, of any threshing nor thrashing nor that either the newspaper or the police chief was unduly alarmed.[44]

The following year, four unrobed and unmasked men placed another Ku Klux Klan wreath at the Washington statue on the morning of his birthday, where several other organizations—including the Masons—had placed similar tributes. The Klan wreath was noticed by the city's parks commissioner who was strolling by. Although he did not order it removed, it had disappeared by lunchtime.[45]

The Newark statue of George Washington where Klansmen laid a wreath that was subsequently removed. *From Joseph Bilby.*

In early April 1923, the first public notice was taken of possible Ku Klux Klan activity in Hudson County. Charles S. Wolf, a post office employee from west New York, was arrested for driving "four or five young men" along the crest of the Palisades where they erected four flaming crosses—an explicitly illegal act in the county. Wolf told police he was asked to become a Klansman but had declined. He also said that his friends were members of the Junior Order of American Mechanics, which was the leading anti-Catholic and anti-immigrant group in America prior to the revival of the Klan.[46]

In May, the Klan announced its presence in Red Bank, sending a donation to the Women's Auxiliary of the American Legion along with a grandiose letterhead reading, "Knights of the Invisible Empire. The Most Sublime Lineage in All History, Commemorating and Perpetuating as It Does the Most Dauntless Organization Known. In the Name of the Fathers—For Our Country, Our Homes and Each Other."[47]

The newspapers had hitherto provided an apparently fair assessment of known Klan activity, which was minimal, despite the organization's attempts to publicize itself toward the end of 1922. By May, however, the Ku Klux Klan launched a new propaganda offensive in the person of a charismatic church lady when Alma White, a bishop no less, publicly endorsed the Klan.

Bishop White had begun life as Mollie Alma Bridwell. She was born in 1862 in Kentucky and converted to Methodism at a local revival meeting in 1878. Bridwell traveled widely, especially for a woman of that era. After attending Millersburg Female College, she visited an aunt in Bannack, Montana, in 1882. Following a stint as a schoolteacher in Bannack, she moved to Salt Lake City, where she taught in a Methodist seminary and married seminarian Kent White—an occasion that facilitated her new identity. She dropped her first name and became Alma White.[48]

The Whites established a church in Denver, but Alma apparently separated from Kent and became estranged from Methodism as well. In 1907, she moved to New Jersey, where she founded the Pillar of Fire Church on a donated farm in the Somerset County community of Zarephath. White was ordained a bishop of her own church by a traveling Methodist evangelist. She then established her own Bible school, Zarephath Academy, on the farm. Zarephath dispatched evangelical recruiters across the country. White's religious community was labeled by a Red Bank, New Jersey newspaper as "an experiment in communism as well as religion" following revival services adherents held at Port Monmouth in 1921.[49]

Bishop White, described by *Time* magazine as having "the mien of an inspired laundress," was a fierce feminist, but only in the service of white Protestant women. She was strongly anti-Catholic, anti-Semitic and anti-immigrant and became a prominent Ku Klux Klan supporter. The Klan reciprocated with generous donations. White believed the Klan would help attain her goal of liberating white Protestant womanhood while keeping minorities and people of other religions "in their place." She praised the organization in her books and pamphlets, including her newsletter, the *Good Citizen*.[50]

Bishop Alma White, described by *Time* magazine as having "the mien of an inspired laundress," was a fierce feminist, but only regarding white Protestant women. *From Joseph Bilby.*

White constantly warned her "100 percent American" readers against the vast international conspiracy that the Catholic Church had launched to take over America. Her evidence was "Rome's idolatrous shrines" that were raising "their towering heads above the din and roar of our great cities, reminding us of the temples of worship in heathen lands." The "costly materials and equipment" needed to build these cathedrals were, in White's fevered imagination, acquired through diversion of funds, beginning with "the great war drives" of the previous decade and continuing through "community chest drives" that had "hoodwinked" gullible Protestants. Alma would set them straight for a mere fifty-cents-a-year subscription to the *Good Citizen*.[51]

White formed a close relationship with Arthur H. Bell, the rising star of the New Jersey Klan. Bell wrote introductions to her books and allegedly wrote a book of his own, entitled *The Ku Klux Klan or the Knights of Columbus Klan: America or Rome*—an anti-Catholic piece that gained popularity in Klan circles—although White may have been the actual author.[52]

A Kleagle, allegedly from New York, visited the Pillar of Fire church on May 1, 1923, no doubt with the belief that it would prove a fertile recruiting ground. Unfortunately for him, word of his appearance got out to the larger community around Bound Brook, and a mob of anti-Klan locals gathered at the venue. The original intent of the protestors seems to have been to heckle the Klan speaker whose opening statement enthusiastically characterized the revived Ku Klux Klan as the "most remarkable movement of modern times."[53]

Bishop White's Zarephath Academy. *From Joseph Bilby.*

The Zarephath Band that occasionally played at Klan events. *From Joseph Bilby.*

Alma White's monthly pro-Klan and anti-Catholic publication, the *Good Citizen*. *From Joseph Bilby*.

The intense hissing and booing that ensued was the first major hostile public reaction to the Klan in New Jersey. The atmosphere deteriorated precipitously, and the meeting turned into a riot in which twenty-five cars were damaged and one hundred "Holy Jumpers" ended up besieged in the "Fiery Temple" under a barrage of stones. Local police and state troopers got the situation under control and hustled church members Elias Horn and Lawrence Winter to the Somerset County jail in Somerville to prevent them from being "lynched by the infuriated mob." More state troopers were rushed to Somerville as another mob began to form near the jail.[54]

Although Pillar of Fire spokesman Reverend A.L. Wolfran, described as the "adjutant" of the church, admitted to a reporter that, as the journalist called them, his "Holy Rollers" completely "endorsed the principles of the Ku Klux Klan," he denied that the Klan speaker had said anything inflammatory to incite the riot. Wolfran tried to frame the occasion as a public service event because "a goodly number of Bound Brook citizens have desired to know the truth about the Ku Klux Klan," and the Pillar of Fire had invited the speaker to help inform the public.[55]

Reverend Wolfran's account was, of course, disputed. Klan opponents told the press that the riot began after the Klan speaker "made several remarks that were interpreted as slurs upon Catholics, Hebrews and Negroes." Father William Fahey, pastor of Saint Joseph's Catholic Church in Bound Brook, denied that he had dispatched anti-Klan demonstrators to Zarephath, "for we have nothing to fear from the Ku Klux Klan." Fahey added that the Kleagle visit to Zarephath had been general knowledge around Bound Brook for four days prior to the event.[56]

A reporter noticed that there was a good deal of Alma White's literature scattered around the scene of the disturbance, including a pamphlet entitled "Ku Klux Klan and Woman's Cause," based on an address she had made the previous December, which praised the Klan as "the prophets of a new and better age." In what seems to be a characteristic silence regarding the Ku Klux Klan in many New Jersey histories, an account of religion in the state published in 1964 makes no mention of the Klan or Alma White's connection with it. The account merely notes that Mrs. White "was a prolific writer, penning many books, magazines, pamphlets and brochures," which were "in large measure responsible for the securing of funds" for her religious colony.[57]

Several days later, a large Klan rally was held at a farm near Bound Brook. Touted as an initiation ceremony, some speculated that it was in response to the anti-Klan activity in the area. Cars approaching the venue reportedly clogged all highways from New Brunswick and Newark. Wary of the previous disaster, Klansmen guarded the approaches, only allowing those with Klan identification to pass.[58]

A reporter allowed to observe from a nearby road described a "horseshoe of headlights" from hundreds of cars forming a protective screen and estimated that twelve thousand Klansmen attended the ceremonies. Incoming cars tried to hide their license plates with handkerchiefs. The gesture was ineffective as reporters were able to identify autos "from Florida, Georgia and other southern states, as well as several western states." It was also noted that "a large number of cars bearing New York plates were permitted to enter the farm." As the night wore on, "Cars from other states, including Massachusetts, Connecticut and Ohio, increased in number, confirming the early reports that it was a national gathering of the Klan." Although local opponents of the Klan became aware of the gathering, they failed to take any action against it.[59]

In Ocean County, the reception was friendlier. On June 5, the Klan held a parade and ceremony at Clark's Landing on the Manasquan River, initiating about two hundred men from Ocean, Monmouth and Middlesex Counties. Three weeks after the debacle at Zarephath, the Central Methodist Episcopal Church on Arnold Avenue in Point Pleasant held a "lodge service," to which organizations with a presence in the town were invited. These included the

"Daughters of Liberty, Daughters of Pocahontas, Eastern Star, Masons, Odd Fellows, Junior Order of American Mechanics, Patriotic Order Sons of America, Red Men, Knights of the Golden Eagle, Knights of Pythias and the Ku Klux Klan."[60]

The Klan received preferential treatment, with fifteen rows of pews reserved. Hooded and robed Klansmen parked their cars along Richmond Avenue and, 109 strong, marched, following American flags and a burning cross, down that street and then Arnold Avenue and into the church, while startled locals gaped at the procession. The costumed Klansmen were accompanied by "Loties, Ladies of the Invisible Empire," as well as two members of the "Royal Riders of the Red Robe," a Klan auxiliary composed of supporters born abroad.[61]

The day's sermon was preached by R.L. Muller of Ocean Grove, who was described as the "supply pastor" of the church. A supply pastor was a lay member appointed to serve a church in a temporary capacity. He could preach, visit the sick and offer some leadership, though he was not ordained or licensed. Muller told reporters afterward, in a refrain that had become common in Klan theatrics, that although he was not a member of the organization, he was "heartily in favor of some of their programs," adding that "any real American should be."[62]

Following the "usual program preceding the sermon," Muller asked innocently if any lodge representative had something to say. Unsurprisingly, a Klansman stood up, approached the pulpit, shook hands with the pastor and thanked him. The Klansman—thought by some to be Arthur Bell—spoke of the organization's principles and "repudiated charges of misconduct on the part of Klansmen."[63]

The hooded spokesman went on to read from a Klan manual that stressed "Americanism, the upholding of the constitution and law and order." He took up a collection among his compatriots and handed it to Muller, who then delivered his sermon, which, according to a member of the press who was present, "did not refer to the Ku Klux Klan either by name or in a veiled manner." Muller later claimed the collection total was "generous." At the end of the service, the Klansmen, described as being from Asbury Park, Belmar, Lakewood and Point Pleasant, marched out to their cars on Richmond Avenue, where they dispersed.[64]

The Klan spokesman's "repudiation of misconduct" was no doubt a reaction to charges that Klansmen had kidnapped and threatened George Titus from nearby West Belmar a few weeks prior to the church service. The eighteen-year-old Titus was forcibly taken from the home of a friend by five armed men and driven in an automobile "through the brush over stumps" to a location on Shark River Hill, where he was subjected to a "terrorizing inquisition" and threatened with dismemberment for allegedly stealing fifty dollars the Klan had donated to his mother. Titus's mother and father were separated, and the Belmar Klavern had given her the money to support herself and her other children.[65]

Titus, who stated that he was never physically harmed, was released by his captors. He denied the theft accusation, and his abduction prompted an investigation by the Monmouth County Prosecutor's Office. As the inquiry proceeded, a letter containing a vigorous denial of the charges arrived at County Detective Charles O. Davenport's office. The correspondence, from an individual described by the press as "Mysterious Mr. Bell," as in the case of the Hall-Mills Murders, mentioned the Klan's purported crime-busting expertise and offered "400 men in three hours" to assist in the investigation. Bell went on to "express the hope that the prosecutor's office would find the offenders and vindicate the Ku Klux Klan of Belmar of connection with the case." The prosecutor did not take up the assistance offer, and there was never any resolution to the incident.[66]

Mysterious Mr. Bell was, of course, Kleagle Arthur H. Bell. Although a Bloomfield resident, Bell was apparently fond of the northern New Jersey shore, where he had personally visited Belmar on several occasions to deliver orders of hoods and robes for local Klansmen.[67]

Bell had likely correctly perceived that, as one newspaper noted, "Monmouth and Ocean Counties are considered as being the center of Ku Klux Klan activity in New Jersey." As a Kleagle of the New Jersey realm, he certainly had access to total membership numbers. In addition, in keeping with his background as a song and dance man, Bell had a good sense of theater and, in his other career as a salesman, knew how to peddle a product. And peddle he did.[68]

The Point Pleasant church appearance was the first in a series of Klan events in the spring and summer of 1923. On Memorial Day, a small group of Klansmen laid "a cross of roses bearing the letters KKK" at the Neptune World War I monument near the Ocean Grove gate. In June, burning crosses appeared in several shore communities, including Point Pleasant and Allenhurst, although it is difficult to determine if these were the work of Klansmen or pranksters. July 4 saw the first crosses burned in Ocean Grove—one near the main gate and another at Fletcher Lake. One Ocean Grove resident yelled, "Look at the Ku Klux Klan fireworks," while another called the fire department. A cross blazed in Belmar near the Shark River

Inlet the same night, and another in Wall Township on Shark River Hill. Flaming crosses also appeared in West Red Bank and Fair Haven and were set alight by persons who fled the scene.[69]

Many years later, Alan Silbergleit, a Jewish resident of Asbury Park, recalled that a cross burning in that city "really shook us up," though he noted, "Some of the most faithful customers of our family's clothing store were 'kluxers' from West Grove." In 2014, the late Fred Byrnes, a retired New Jersey National Guard sergeant major, recalled to author Joseph Bilby that his Irish Catholic grandmother told him that she had rented an outbuilding on her Ocean County farm to some Klansmen for a meeting in the 1920s. When Byrnes told her that he found that hard to understand, considering their pronounced anti-Catholicism, she said she did not care, "since their money was green," and they never bothered her. In Bergen County, robed Klansmen reportedly purchased their cigarettes in a Jewish-owned store. These stories add to the bark-versus-bite narrative of the New Jersey Klan.[70]

In at least one case in 1922, the opposite was stated. William Currie, a hardware store owner in Roselle, claimed that his "business had suffered because of stories he is a member of the Ku Klux Klan." He told a reporter that a town resident had sent him a letter reading, "Enclosed is balance which I owe you. This ends all business deals with you because I am an American, and a good one. I hope. I do not care to do business with anyone who is affiliated with a non-American organization such as the Ku Klux Klan." Currie denied any connection with the Klan and pointed out that his wife was Catholic, and he would not even be eligible for membership since he was born in Ireland.[71]

Although not actually violent, cross burning could certainly be threatening. Bergen County Klansmen erected a metal cross wrapped in gasoline-soaked burlap on the lawn of Italian immigrant Vincent Orfini—an artist and part-time railroad worker who had recently moved to Hillsdale from New York City. They then set the cross on fire, terrifying Orfini's wife and children. Although no physical harm was done to the family, the incident enraged Vincent, who was working at the time. The following morning, he encountered Klansman Albert Rawson in a local hardware store, demanding, "What the hell did you think you were doing last night? You scared my wife half to death!" Orfini, normally a peaceful soul, then purchased a rifle and pistol at the store, which was no doubt noted by Rawson. The family was never harassed again. The Rawsons, like many in the New Jersey Klan, appear to have been more interested in self-promotional theater than in actual violence.[72]

It wasn't all cross burnings and fun for Klansmen. A Maryland newspaper reported that on June 26, Reverend DeWitt Cobb hosted a small Klan parade in Asbury Park, where some residents were no doubt nostalgic for the good old days of Methodist founder James Bradley. Times had changed, and reaction was swift. The paper noticed that sixty Klan members marching in full regalia to the church were attacked by a mob in a "free-for-all fight" in which "several Klansmen were thrown to the street" before police separated them from the anti-Klan demonstrators. The Asbury Park Klan got no support from Mayor Clarence Hetrick, who governed with the support of African American, Catholic and Jewish voters and the local business community.[73]

On July 9, 1923, there was another house of worship visit, this time to the Harmony Church in Adelphia, where Reverend Otis F. VanBrunt was holding a service honoring "old soldiers and Spanish-American War veterans." Forty-two Klansmen marched in to the tune of the "Star-Spangled Banner" and contributed to the collection. Interestingly, the New Jersey Spanish War Veterans state commander had characterized the Klan as "a white robed invisible menace" at the organization's June convention in Asbury Park. On

The First Baptist Church in Asbury Park that was the scene of an attack on Klansmen. *From Joseph Bilby.*

July 29, fifty-six hooded and robed Klan members attended services at the First Methodist Episcopal Church in Sea Bright, arriving in automobiles bearing placards reading, "We Stand by the Law."[74]

Arthur Bell, now the "Grand Titan" in charge of the central New Jersey Klan, held an initiation ceremony in Allenwood and invited a reporter. The affair, no doubt carefully prepared, featured the standard circle of cars, their headlights directed at an altar and cross in the middle of a field in which an estimated 750 Klansmen chanted as 300 initiates, or "aliens," as they were called, filed into the circle. The ceremony ended with all who were present kneeling for a prayer as the cross burst into flames. While the cross burned, Bell hawked tickets to an Asbury Park concert, allegedly for the benefit of blind children. If nothing else, the former vaudevillian had brought outdoor theater to Monmouth County.[75]

On July 15, there was a Klan wedding in Mantoloking, with a procession of seventy-five "Loties," who marched into the West Presbyterian Church. The ladies were attired in "white silk dresses, in a kimono-like style, with red, white and blue cord around the waist…and a harem veil and draped headdress with a red, white and blue band with L.O.T.I.E. in gold letters." The leader of the "Ladies of the Invisible Empire" explained their principles as: "Free speech, free press, free public schools, white supremacy and separation of church and state."[76]

The trope that the Ku Klux Klan was for separation of church and state was a consistent one for the organization, even though the Klan also demanded that the government declare the United States a "Christian Nation" and that the Christian Bible be taught in public schools. This ironic "Christian Nationalist" belief appeared often in the past and has had periodic resurgences even to the present day, though occasionally with different targets.

The grandest event of the summer was staged near the Monmouth County community of Farmingdale. On August 24, "several thousand" Klansmen gathered in a field adjacent to "the main road to the shore" (today's Route 33). Since there was no one available with the expertise to accurately measure a crowd, it is likely that the attendance information, as in other cases, was exaggerated by a Klan representative.[77]

A newspaper noted that the Klan had "deviated from its regular custom and allowed word of the proposed demonstration to gain rather widespread circulation." Klansmen "wore their white hoods and gowns and a huge blazing cross illuminated the scene and also served to attract great throngs of additional spectators." The crowd of the curious created the impression that the event was even larger than it would have been if it had been limited to the true believers.[78]

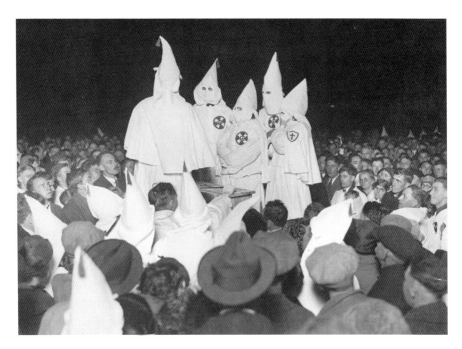

Klan wedding on the beach at Point Pleasant. *From Newark, New Jersey Public Library.*

Ladies of the Invisible Empire, a group later renamed "Kamelia." *From Joseph Bilby.*

Although the event was billed as a Monmouth and Ocean County affair, there were reports that many Klan members coming from the north drove through New Brunswick on their way to the event. It is quite likely that Bell, the professional huckster, got as many Klansmen as he could to travel to Farmingdale to expand the crowd even further.[79]

And then came trouble. For some reason, perhaps a feeling that their star was on the rise, the Monmouth County Klansmen (mostly from Asbury Park and Belmar) decided to hold a meeting in August in Perth Amboy. This was a city with a large number of immigrants—one estimate has it that 72 percent of the city's population was born abroad. The Klan scheduled the gathering, which had been "widely advertised," for the Odd Fellows Hall on Smith Street in the center of the city.[80]

They should have taken heed from the results of a previous recruiting rally in Perth Amboy. On June 4, the Junior Order of American Mechanics Hall on Smith Street had hosted out-of-state Kleagle Reverend Oscar Haywood. One hundred robed Klansmen were present, and a throng of five hundred demonstrators angry at the Klan's anti-Catholic and anti-Jewish rhetoric gathered outside. The protestors rushed the hall, the meeting was cancelled and Haywood, who had been declaring that Catholics and Jews were "not true Americans," led his audience in a hasty exit out the back door while city police officers held off the crowd. Ku Kluxers were generally not welcome in the urban centers north of the Raritan River, and parading Klansmen were the target of an egg barrage in Bloomfield on June 15.[81]

Apparently oblivious to those harbingers, two hundred Klansmen arrived in full hooded regalia at the Perth Amboy venue in the early evening of August 30. Almost immediately, a hostile crowd, which swelled to an estimated five thousand, began to gather outside. Urged by their leaders to attack the hall, the mob surged forward, hurling bricks. The Klan meeting broke up immediately, and Klansmen trying to flee the site via fire escapes and windows were badly beaten. Officials desperately tried to restore order as the entire Perth Amboy police force along with the city's fire department rushed to the scene. Officers fired guns in the air, threw tear gas bombs and wielded clubs while firemen turned their hoses on the crowd. The attackers cut the hose lines and pushed the police back into the building.[82]

Klansmen lucky enough to escape the initial onslaught ripped off their robes and headed for the woods that surrounded the city. The arrival of state police prompted a lull in the fighting, which enabled officers to load Klan members into a patrol wagon and attempt to drive them away. The mob

Downtown Perth Amboy in the 1920s. *From Joseph Bilby.*

surged forward again and overturned the vehicle, spilling out the occupants and resuming the assault.[83]

At five o'clock the following morning, the police tried to discreetly escort the few remaining Klan members out of town. A group of one hundred or more rioters who had lingered overnight attacked the departing Klansmen, however, and administered "heavy beatings" that left some hospitalized. One was saved from being tossed into the Perth Amboy sewer system via an open manhole by a police officer who shouted, "My God. Don't do that. It's murder." John Megill of Farmingdale was chased through the streets and took refuge in the Perth Amboy police headquarters until his brother drove to the city the following day to bring him home. There were only three arrests during the entire incident—all Klan members charged with carrying concealed weapons without a permit. A grand jury failed to indict anyone. Retreating Klansmen yelled at their pursuers that they "would be back ten thousand strong" and were answered with, "And there will be twenty thousand waiting for you."[84]

Joseph M. "Marty" Boa of Shrewsbury, whose grandparents lived in Long Branch in the 1920s, recalls his grandmother telling him that a friend tried to recruit his grandfather into the Klan, describing it as a fraternal social club. She told Marty that she told her husband, "No way," and he obeyed her wishes. She continued, "Soon after, they all went up to Perth Amboy to chase Catholics and got beat up. So, I was right." A prescient lady.[85]

A few days later, the *Newark Ledger* concluded editorially what should have occurred to the Klansmen before they made their chimerical foray into Middlesex County:

> *New Jersey is not a healthy place for the Klan. That has been demonstrated by attacks upon the sheeted order members in various places, of which the second one at Perth Amboy was the climax to date. This state has a very large proportion of its population consisting of the racial and religious elements to which the Klan is hostile. All of these people are not going to sit quietly and watch a secret society which is causing a reign of terror and lawlessness in many sections develop and flaunt itself here.... Those who are sowing the wind already get the whirlwind in New Jersey all right.*[86]

Yet another Klan defeat occurred in the tumultuous year of 1923. Atlantic City, a cosmopolitan resort, was the site. In addition to the beach and family fun, Atlantic City was known for illegal gambling, brothels and speakeasies and was a major "rum running" destination for smuggled alcohol during prohibition. It also had a large African American population that worked in the city's hotels and voted for the candidates of legendary Republican Atlantic County political boss Enoch "Nucky" Johnson.

In January, Christopher Carvis, manager of the Garden Inn Hotel on South New York Avenue, a popular speakeasy that had been raided as a "disorderly house" (euphemism for brothel), received an almost polite demand that he "please stop bootlegging and run a decent place." The notice was signed "K.K.K." and bore the letterhead of Klan headquarters in Atlanta. James Lightfoot, an African American attorney who opposed Klan-supported formalized school segregation, had received a similar missive asking him to desist. There is no indication that either man complied.[87]

The city by the sea's mayor was Edward L. Bader, a Catholic, which did not bode well for Klan activities. The local Klavern, which claimed an unlikely membership of four thousand, announced in the state Klan newsletter, *The New Jersey Fiery Cross*, that a parade was planned through the city's streets "even at the price of bloodshed, if necessary." The bold proclamation quickly elicited a response from Mayor Bader and the Atlantic City Council. On November 22, without specifically mentioning the Klan, the council passed an ordinance prohibiting "the parading or

Mayor Edward L. Bader of Atlantic City, seen here with the first Miss America, Margaret Gorman, signed an ordinance prohibiting "the parading or assembling of persons disguising their identity and the burning of fiery crosses in the city" in November 1923. *From Joseph Bilby.*

assembling of persons disguising their identity and the burning of fiery crosses." There was also a move within the city to create an anti-Klan vigilante force of Catholics and African Americans with an abundance of potential volunteers. The Atlantic City chapter of the Elks fraternal organization moved to expel Klan members from its ranks. Elk Exalted Ruler and Atlantic City attorney Eugene Schwinghammer stated that "the principles and practices of the Ku Klux Klan are in direct variance to the precepts on which the Order of Elks was founded."[88]

The Klan responded with its usual anonymous bluster, claiming that it had the power to swing elections in Atlantic City. A cross was burned on the beach, but the fire was extinguished by "Walter Castor, a Negro policeman on beat," while another officer, Paul Jones, stood by, revolver in hand, although whoever set the cross afire did not wait around. A crowd of the curious gathered, but there were no further disturbances. A rumor began to spread that "Negroes in the north side of town have stored away, for an emergency, three machine guns to protect themselves in the event of a Klan visit." There would be no visit, and there would be no electoral victory for the Klan—once more demonstrating that grandiloquent threats were usually no more than hollow rants.

The Klan presence in Atlantic County seems to have been concentrated in Pleasantville and nearby Northfield. In 1924, the burial of Atlantic and Cape May County Kleagle Andrew Andridge in Pleasantville drew several hundred robed and hooded male and female participants. A newspaper report noted that "Klansmen and women marched in full regalia but with their faces bare." Because the funeral service prior to interment was held at the First Presbyterian Church in Atlantic City, it is likely that hoods were raised to comply with the 1923 ordinance.[89]

In a 1925 lawsuit, an unsuccessful freeholder primary candidate alleged that two men assaulted him outside the election venue in Northfield. Jurors were questioned about their affiliation with the Klan. They all denied membership, giving rise to the probability that the attackers, who were found liable and had to pay $500 each to the man bringing the suit, were suspected Klansmen, although they were not dressed in Klan regalia.[90]

A Ku Klux Klan parade in Northfield, New Jersey, in the 1920s. *From the Northfield Cultural Committee and the Northfield, New Jersey Museum.*

An improvised float in the Northfield Klan parade. *From the Northfield Cultural Committee and the Northfield, New Jersey Museum.*

Unlike in many states, particularly Indiana and even Colorado, New Jersey's political leadership disdained the Klan. Governor George Silzer roundly condemned the organization in a speech at an Atlantic City banquet on September 8. Silzer declared,

> *Of all the undemocratic and un-American organizations, the Ku Klux Klan is the worst. It fosters violence and I tell you that any group which does that is breeding trouble for the country and the world. I was asked by Klansmen why they were not protected when they held their meetings and I replied that I could pay no more attention to masked faces than I could to anonymous letters. We cannot permit this hidden army to work havoc in our country.*[91]

For the most part, the state's journalists seemed to agree with Silzer. In addition to editorial disapproval of the Klan, the *Newark Evening News* regularly reported Klan misadventures and problems, not only in New Jersey, but across the country. This included an attempt in Oklahoma to pass legislation making it a "misdemeanor to wear masks" and the arrest of Caleb

New Jersey governor George
Sebastian Silzer. *From Joseph Bilby.*

Ridley, the Klan's "Imperial Kludd," in Atlanta on the charge of "being drunk and driving an automobile."[92]

On October 16, however, the New Jersey Ku Klux Klan was granted a corporate charter by the state's attorney general, over a legal protest from Newark attorney William J. McFadden, who stated that the organization "openly discriminates against a race that forms an integral part of the citizenship." The attorney general responded that the application was in "proper legal form" and that that was enough.[93]

A patriotic service held at a Baptist church in Middletown in December drew about seventy-five Red Bank Klansmen, each of whom donated a dollar to the pastor, Reverend F.R. Shermer, who unsurprisingly praised the organization. One Klansman, identified as Mr. Baker of Spring Lake, explained that Klan members had to wear hoods for "self-protection," since some who had marched hoodless in a parade in a northern New Jersey town had been fired from their jobs.[94]

It had been a long year for the New Jersey Klan, but "Mysterious Mr. Bell," now out in the open, had plans and returned to Monmouth County for another church show. On December 9, Bell marshaled members of the Ku Klux Klan, Royal Riders of the Red Robe and the Knights of the Kamelia (female Klanspeople) in full regalia to march into Asbury Park's First Baptist Church auditorium to the tune of "Onward, Christian Soldiers." This delighted the seven hundred members of the congregation who were residents of both Asbury Park and Ocean Grove, and who provided a "warm welcome."[95]

A reporter's analysis revealed that there were "Seventy-four Klansmen, 41 'lady knights' and 20 Royal Riders" in the group, and this time there were no hecklers to put up with. Bell mounted a flag-bedecked stage, unmasked and delivered an address on the Klan's "policy and motives." He "denied that the K.K.K. was anti-Jew, Negro or Catholic and declared that the public opinion that branded them as tar and feather specialists was the result of notorious abuses on the part of the press." He added that, in fact, the Klan did much to help "these classes" but did not admit them to membership because the Klan was a "pro-Protestant and pro-American organization" and that those causes were "not properly supported by these racial and religious groups." Bell's seemingly soft rhetoric followed instructions from Imperial Wizard Evans, who had advised Klansmen to "not abuse the enemy" in any forum where a published quote might make the organization look bad. In closed session, of course, they could rant about the dangers of "the enemy" as much as they wished.[96]

Grand Titan Bell went on, however, to rant about "race mixing," a paranoid fantasy the Klan obsessed over and deplored as a road to the United States becoming a "nation run by mongrels." Bell said he had somehow discovered "eighty-seven thousand cases of white girls living with Negroes and men of the yellow race." He had concluded from this that "members of Negro societies had pledged to marry white girls" and had gone on to accuse Catholics of planning a military coup and Jews of taking over "finance and the law." The latter was an echo of Henry Ford's distribution of the bogus *Protocols of the Elders of Zion*. After his oration, Bell was warmly applauded by the audience, while Reverend David A. MacMurray assured the public that the country had nothing to fear from the Klan, which was using a vigilante allusion—an organization dedicated to "cleaning things up in America." What that meant in detail went unsaid.[97]

CHAPTER 4

"THE CHARGE THAT A NUDE WOMAN SAT ON MY LAP IS A DAMNABLE LIE."

Prior to 1924, the New Jersey Ku Klux Klan's center was rural Somerset County. As Arthur Bell began to assume control of the state organization, however, he started shifting Klan activities south to Monmouth County, where the year had ended with his great reception in Asbury Park.

Bell apparently perceived the Monmouth County communities along Raritan Bay as a region with much Klan potential. In early January 1924, there was a Klan meeting at Highlands Methodist Church in the Bayshore community of Atlantic Highlands. About one hundred costumed Klansmen attended the gathering with an estimated seven hundred curious residents gathering inside and outside of the church. Bell was accompanied by his wife, Leah, in Kamelia garb, and promised, in his standard self-righteous style, to "clean up the bootleg business" along the bay. The implied threat of vigilante action had by now become a staple of the Klan's "public service" announcements. Following Bell's opening address, Belmar Klan leader J.B. Baker advised the audience that "we know the conditions here. We know the rum-runners and bootleggers are buying politicians. We are going to see that this is cleaned up."[98]

The Bayshore was indeed a problematic area. The region's attraction as a tourist destination and commercial fishing mecca had been spoiled by raw sewage combined with other residue drifting from the cities to the north, particularly New York City. Oil slicks and debris turned one section of the Bayshore into an area known as the "mud hole," and the stench from rotting garbage and dead animals along certain beaches was horrendous. The environmental degradation cost jobs, but as the saying goes, nature abhors a vacuum.

Prohibition provided new employment and business opportunities. Bootlegging boomed, and the area became a major smuggling point for the importation and distribution of alcoholic beverages. Liquor-laden ships anchored offshore at "rum row," the international three-mile limit. Fishing boat captains, now known as "rumrunners," sailed their smaller crafts out to load liquor and ran them back to shore. They primarily returned to Atlantic Highlands, although cargoes landed all along the Bayshore as opportunities arose. The captains received five dollars (sixty dollars with 2016 inflation) per run, and the laborers were paid one dollar (twelve dollars) for unloading the boats and another dollar for loading the smuggled alcohol onto trucks that whisked it away for distribution.[99]

Many bootleggers, including mobsters Al Lillien and Vito Genovese, were Jewish or Italian immigrants or sons of immigrants, as were the hijackers attracted to Bayshore communities by the illegal liquor trade. Rival gangs exchanged gunfire in the streets of Atlantic Highlands, where law enforcement was thwarted by local officials, including the chief of police, who was believed to be on the mob payroll. The sizable Italian immigrant community in Atlantic Highlands, most of whom resided near St. Agnes Roman Catholic Church in the less-prosperous west end, helped form a nearly complete set of declared Klan enemies along the Bayshore. The area seemed natural for Arthur Bell's "clean-up" rhetoric.[100]

In many ways, Bell's pledge was a joke. For Klansmen to hint at taking matters into their own hands to "clean up" was pretty much a work of fiction in the same vein as Bell's promises to help solve murders like the Hall-Mills case. Vigilantism had been roundly condemned by New Jersey public officials, from the governor down, and the state's working- and middle-class, Protestant Bible–spouting Klan membership was a poor match for murderous gangsters armed with Thompson submachine guns.

Although they were involved in police and vigilante actions in other states, particularly Indiana and in the South, there is no evidence of the Ku Klux Klan either aiding law enforcement or acting as a private police force in New Jersey. In his book, *The Ku Klux Klan in the City*, Kenneth Jackson cites a 1924 letter to United States attorney general Harlan Stone as the source for his account of the "Camden County Rangers," an alleged Klan-sponsored organization "wearing United States Army uniforms with Klan insignia" that "patrolled the public highways to prevent parking by lovers." There is no mention of such an organization in any New Jersey newspapers, and it was likely yet another fictional force of the Klan.[101]

Elsewhere in the United States, this was not the case. In Indiana, Grand Dragon David Curtis "Steve" Stephenson revitalized and funded an obsolete vigilante organization that was founded in 1845 as the Horse Thief Detective Association, but participation had dwindled with the rise of automotive transportation. The group still existed as a sort of Caucasian fraternal order, which made the Klan appealing to many members. The "detectives" were legally appointed constables and possessed the power to arrest. In 1922 and 1923, members of that force, using questionable tactics such as the indiscriminate stop and search of automobiles, arrested and turned in three thousand individuals for prosecution. This established an Indiana Klan reputation for enforcing "law and order," although evidence suggests that most of the confiscated liquor was imbibed by Klansmen.[102]

The Indiana example would not fly in New Jersey, where law enforcement was not complicit with vigilantes. What Bell promoted was a private version of the World War I snoopers hired by the Bureau of Investigation to report on alleged disloyal Americans. As part of his continuing quest for public approval of the Klan as a civic organization, he had previously claimed that his secret agents were instrumental in a series of bootleg liquor raids across Monmouth and Ocean Counties. Bell's burgeoning faux credentials, however, were being exposed for what they were—wild exaggerations at best. In 1923, when federal agents arrested bootleggers and confiscated alcohol in Belmar, Lakewood and Point Pleasant, the state prohibition head strongly denied "that evidence for raids in Monmouth County was secured by the Ku Klux Klan." A sympathetic local Methodist minister admitted that "although the Klan stands for law enforcement," there was indeed no evidence of Klan involvement in the raids.

Where the Klan did succeed in the Bayshore and other Monmouth County communities was in driving off African American, Catholic and Jewish vacationers and influencing a few local elections. Rumrunning, for all of Bell's self-promotion, went on unabated until the end of prohibition in the next decade, and the bootleggers were in far more danger from Coast Guardsmen, prohibition agents and each other than they were from the Klan.[103]

Another Monmouth County "clean-up" attempt that failed dismally occurred in Asbury Park. Clarence Hetrick was not only the mayor of Asbury Park but also president of the city's chamber of commerce. He was perfectly suited for the job as the biggest booster of Asbury's transition

Asbury Park mayor Clarence Hetrick. *From Joseph Bilby.*

from a nineteenth-century Methodist vacation spot a little less tight laced than Ocean Grove into a modern resort and local economic center. It was Hetrick's cozy relationship with the Asbury Park business community that provided an opportunity for the Klan, allied with the city's religious old guard, to attempt a coup that would remove him from office on charges of immoral activity.

In April 1924, the mayor attended the city's annual business show—a trade fair held at the Boardwalk Casino. The event featured one hundred exhibitors, all of whom were dedicated to advertising and expanding the growing consumer-oriented retail economy of the 1920s. On the evening the show closed, the mayor enjoyed a "dinner and cabaret entertainment" at the nearby Deal Inn, a well-known speakeasy, with leading Asbury Park and Monmouth County merchants and political leaders. Following the event, Walter Tindall, a resident of Ocean Grove and an Asbury Park print shop owner, claimed it had turned into an orgy in which he had refused to participate. Tindall was likely one of "several local people" previously reported as covert Klansmen, and his statement instantly galvanized the Civic Church League and the Ku Klux Klan against the mayor. According

DEAL INN AND COTTAGES - DEAL BEACH, N.J.

The Deal Inn, site of the party that the Klan used to attack Mayor Hetrick. *From Joseph Bilby.*

to Tindall's account, there was "much drinking" at the affair, and "five women imported from New York gave an improper display."[104]

Klan members immediately convened a meeting in Long Branch to denounce Hetrick. The Klan proposed, with its usual bombast, to organize a committee to "begin cleaning up the coast resort cities." There seemed to be close coordination between the pronouncements of the Klan and the Asbury Park clergy, as the "orgy" was simultaneously damned from Protestant pulpits across the city. On April 6, the ministers placed a notice in the *Asbury Park Press,* announcing that at church meetings that evening, the city's clergy would roundly condemn the Deal Inn party, using the Tindall statement as the theme of their sermons. Methodist pastor Reverend Furman A. DeMaris, who admitted that he had conferred with Klansmen before orating on the matter, vowed that "if only one tenth of the charges made in this affidavit are true, it would be time to take drastic action." Indeed, DeMaris welcomed Klan support to "clean up" the city. Baptist minister David A. MacMurray opined that political officeholders attending an event at which "whiskey, champagne and beer flowed" and where the entertainment "was characterized by lewdness, should be driven from office." The clergymen handed Tindall's affidavit over to the Monmouth County prosecutor for grand jury presentment.[105]

The interior of the Deal Inn, where the alleged incident of a nude woman sitting on Mayor Hetrick's lap occurred. *From Joseph Bilby.*

Mayor Hetrick vigorously denied the accusations. The mayor stated that "any allegation to the effect that nude women were present is a lie pure and simple" and emphatically declared, "The charge that a nude woman sat on my lap is a damnable lie." In any event, the charges collapsed when no one corroborated Tindall's accusations, and he was revealed as an apparently bankrupt Klan puppet of Arthur Bell. One account noted that Tindall was reportedly in hiding at Bell's home. The *Asbury Park Press* speculated on whether the county grand jury was going to consider Tindall "a veracious citizen, a prude, or just a plain liar." Tindall's comeuppance was not long as his account was summarily dismissed, and he was charged with perjury. In August, Tindall was also charged with issuing a "worthless check." The Monmouth County Jewish community noted that since many of Asbury Park's business owners were Jewish, and the Klan was involved, there may well have been an additional motive for the charges. The mayor's triumph broke the back of the Klan in Asbury Park.[106]

In the middle of the Klan's shore "clean-up" campaign, the organization was tagged as a threat to public safety in a *Newark News* editorial. The paper suggested that, since the forest fire season was approaching, "it might as well be recognized now that the burning of crosses by Ku Klux Klansmen is going to provide an additional hazard this year." The paper claimed that the burning of two crosses near Dover may well have been responsible for a fire that "burned over 200 square feet of underbrush" and stated that cross burners deserved "prompt prosecution."[107]

Arthur Bell, who now claimed to be the District Kleagle for Middlesex, Monmouth and Ocean Counties, and no doubt hoped for a rebound from some rocky publicity, planned a massive public event for the Fourth of July weekend in 1924. There were similar gatherings in other locations across the country as well, as the Klan pushed its "America First" allegedly patriotic agenda. Before proceeding, however, Bell needed a venue. This came about through the efforts of two Klan representatives, Oliver G. Frake of Red Bank and J. William Jones of Long Branch, who had negotiated to purchase the Elkwood Park land in Long Branch. Today, the property (in Oceanport) is the site of Monmouth Park racetrack. Ironically, the city of Long Branch had been the sin center of the north Jersey Shore in the late nineteenth century.[108]

Elkwood Park began in the 1890s as a private racetrack and shotgun target-shooting venue, which included clay bird and live pigeon shoots for wealthy patrons. The 130-acre park was complete with a "fine residence" and outbuildings, all surrounded by an iron fence, and went through several financial crises and owners. By 1924, the property was owned by Frederick Lewisohn, reportedly a "Wall Street banker," although the actual deed cited him as a "lunatic" and was signed by his "guardian," Maurice J. Cross. Frake and Jones and their wives incorporated as the Imperial Social Club and officially acquired the property on June 20, 1924, with a $130,000 mortgage. They later transferred the land to a new corporation, the Elkwood Park Association. In late June, Elkwood was busy. The *New York Times* reported, "Day and night since Saturday, mechanics and laborers have been at work transforming the 130-acre tract into a place for the reception of thousands of visitors."[109]

The occasion they were anticipating was Bell's "tri-state convention of Klansmen from New Jersey, Delaware and Eastern Pennsylvania," which also attracted "hooded knights from New York, Connecticut and the national headquarters." Reporters were told the event would include a massive parade of Klansmen in full regalia, with "mounted officers, several bands and many floats" through Long Branch, followed by "outdoor sports, fireworks and dancing." For evening entertainment, they were promised initiations of "Klansmen, Royal Red Riders, junior Klansmen and a massive night time ceremony." There would also be Klan weddings, Klan christenings and drill team demonstrations from the New Jersey Kavaliers. To drum up local support, Bell and his wife appeared before a Sunday service crowd

A brochure advertising the "Tri-state Klonklave" held at Elkwood Park in July 1924. *From Moss Collection, Monmouth University Library.*

Left: A photo of Arthur Bell used in the brochure advertising the "Tri-State Klonklave." *From Moss Collection, Monmouth University Library.*

Right: A photo of a "flapperish" Leah Bell used in the brochure advertising the "Tri-State Klonklave." *From Moss Collection, Monmouth University Library.*

of four thousand at the Ocean Grove auditorium, declaring that the Klan was "a band of Christian and patriotic white men and women, 100 percent Americans."[110]

The press was told there would be parking available for twenty thousand cars and that forty thousand people would participate in the celebration—a number that was escalated to fifty thousand and then eighty thousand. The celebration was labeled as both a "Klorero" and a "Klonklave," and Klan officials told reporters that the event would be "the largest ever held in the United States." The actual affair, as was usually the case, differed markedly from the predictions of the public relations blitz that preceded it.

According to reporters who were allowed access to the park prior to the induction ceremonies, the actual number of attendees, including family members and the curious, was "between 20,000 and 30,000." Even so, Bell had succeeded in creating a significant Klan showing in Monmouth County.[111]

Although the theme of the festivities was ostensibly "religious and political freedom," it turned into a "Krusade" against Irish Catholic New

The parking area at the Elkwood Park event. *From Randall Gabrielan.*

York governor Alfred E. Smith, who was viewed as a potential Democratic presidential candidate in 1924. The crowd "howlingly endorsed" a speaker's declaration that "no one but a Protestant will ever sit in the White House." Although Bell would later deny it, there was apparently a carnival game in which customers could "hurl balls at an effigy of Governor Smith." A placard over the governor's form advised, "Keep Al Smith out of the White House. Three shots for a nickel." There was also a report that some $30,000 in refreshment coupons were stolen by persons unknown, which was hotly denied by a Klan representative who identified himself as a district Kleagle known as George.[112]

The highlight of the entire event was the afternoon march down Broadway. The parade was led by a mounted, robed Klansman with a green sash and featured three bands and floats from "a dozen Monmouth County towns." A reporter noted that Freehold's "Molly Pitcher float" had a "slight historical inaccuracy. One of the Continental soldiers was dressed in the uniform of a Union soldier in the Civil War." The reporter was likely in error himself, though, since the Monmouth battleground was later the site of a Civil War camp. Another float featured a Liberty Bell with a Boy Scout holding a placard that read, "We want the Holy Bible in our Schools." Of course, he did not mean the Catholic version, and a speaker earlier in the day had attacked parochial schools as un-American.[113]

This page, top: The concession stand area at the 1924 Tri-state Klonklave. *From Randall Gabrielan.*

This page, bottom: The Red Bank Klan band tunes up at Elkwood Park for a parade in Long Branch in July 1924. *From Randall Gabrielan.*

Opposite: Klansmen getting ready to move out of Elkwood Park for the Long Branch parade. *From Randall Gabrielan.*

The sidewalks along the line of the march were packed with spectators, both supporters and opponents who were generally orderly, save for an occasional firecracker. There was some clapping and a bit of booing, but things remained calm for the most part. Although Klan leaders had predicted "fifteen thousand or more" marchers, and a fawning article likely written by a Klansman in a local weekly newspaper reported that "between seven thousand and eight thousand participated," Long Branch chief of police William D. Walling estimated the actual number of parade participants at three thousand two hundred. One most likely apocryphal account of the spectacle that has endured in Monmouth County folklore is that some nuns from a nearby Catholic school who were watching the procession identified one hooded participant, by his shoes, as either their iceman or butcher and subsequently canceled his contract.[114]

How many of the marching Klansmen were truly from New Jersey is unknown. A New Brunswick newspaper reported that "large numbers" of Klan members, many from New York, drove through the city on their way south the day prior to the parade. Some of the cars bore banners emblazoned with "KKK." The cars were "met with jeers" from locals, and one automobile was bombarded with "a shower of brick-bats, bricks and bottles."[115]

The merchants of Long Branch were not happy with the aftermath of the Klonvocation. A retrospective in 1940 noted, perhaps with a bit of

The Klan parades down Broadway in Long Branch in July 1924. *From Ocean Township, New Jersey Historical Society.*

exaggeration, "The effect on Long Branch business was disastrous. The Jewish summer residents departed from the town the next day, practically *en masse*, leaving a deserted city of ruined shopkeepers and empty hotels and boarding houses. Members of the Negro population locked their doors and refused to emerge on the street for several days. Similarly, Catholics, for whose benefit several fiery crosses had been burned, either left the community or took steps to protect themselves."[116]

Although pleased with the Long Branch publicity, by August, the Klan was again on the public relations defensive. This was the case within the boundaries of Asbury Park, where a reporter had interviewed the vacationing Thomas Dixon. Dixon's novel, *The Clansman*, had provided the inspiration for D.W. Griffith's *The Birth of a Nation*. The author, living in New York on the considerable fortune he had garnered from the book and film, unhesitatingly condemned the current Klan as "a growing menace to the cause of law and order." He also made clear he

Democratic presidential candidate John W. Davis and his vice-presidential running mate Charles W. Bryan in Sea Girt, New Jersey, in August 1924. *From National Guard Militia Museum of New Jersey.*

had refused an offer to join the organization and characterized the Klan as "a menace to American democracy."

In August, Democratic presidential candidate John W. Davis, a prominent New York attorney who had previously been ambivalent regarding the Ku Klux Klan, gave a speech that left no doubt he was anti-Klan. He delivered this message at a rally held by New Jersey governor Silzer at the New Jersey National Guard Camp at Sea Girt. The camp also served as the governor's summer quarters and was in the heart of the Klan's Monmouth County stronghold.[117]

Within a few weeks, perhaps inspired by newspaper reports of the grand celebration in Long Branch, burning crosses appeared around the midnight hour in various places in Bridgewater. As was often the case, whether they were placed there by Klansmen or by pranksters was unknown, as the perpetrators fled the scene.[118]

Despite Arthur Bell's goodwill propaganda offensive, outside the shore area, the feeling regarding the Klan in New Jersey remained more hostile than not. On July 28, Trenton's chief of police denied a Klan organizer's application for a permit to conduct a Labor Day parade in the state capital. The chief told the Klansman that neither he nor any city official had the authority to grant such a permit to any group wearing masks. He went on to say that "in view of the feeling in this city on the activities of the order, bloodshed might result from a public parade or demonstration."[119]

Denied Trenton, the Klan secured a permit from neighboring Hamilton Township. On Labor Day, according to one newspaper report, ten thousand Klansmen and family members from fourteen states, as far away as Oklahoma and Indiana, camped at Springdale Park in the township and then held a parade, protected by local and state police. Following the parade, which skirted the border between Trenton and Hamilton, there were two Klan marriages and fifty Klan baptisms. There were no disturbances during the day, even though a number of African American Trentonians gathered to watch the Klansmen march by at the city border. That night, however, "Klan enemies," likely from Trenton, slipped into the parking lot and slashed the tires of one hundred automobiles.[120]

In September 1924, the Paterson Klan chapter made another attempt at relevance with its usual tactic of public pronouncements. During one of the city's seemingly endless succession of mill worker strikes, the mayor called for deportation of people he called "foreign agitators" among the strikers. The local Klan quickly chimed in, demanding that the workers end "their brazen, open arrogant and defiant slap at Americanism in this community." Court and police pressure collapsed the strike, but there is little doubt the Klansmen patted themselves on the back for their contribution.[121]

With calm returned by autumn, the Klan resumed visiting churches. On October 26, about three hundred robed and hooded Klan men and women, led by Arthur and Leah Bell and accompanied by a band, attended a service at the West Grove Methodist Episcopal Church in Neptune. Reverend A.J. Messler addressed the congregation on "Americanism" while the Bells lectured a crowd of the curious that had gathered outside the church.[122]

That November, the New Jersey Klan supported the Republican Party, although the party's state and national candidates disassociated themselves from the endorsement in New Jersey. In North Bergen, "men and women in Ku Klux Klan costumes distributed leaflets favoring the Republican national, state and local tickets after services in the First Baptist Church." With the headline, "Danger! Danger!" the leaflets called for "good government." They endorsed all Republican candidates from Calvin Coolidge down the ticket, save for "Isidore Sworkin, a Hoboken lawyer running for the New Jersey Assembly, and Dominick B. Elia, a candidate for Registrar from West Hoboken," most likely for religious or ethnic reasons, as their names signaled probable "non-Protestant."[123]

CHAPTER 5

"YOU WILL FIND HER AT MILFORD, PENNSYLVANIA, WITH THAT SCOUNDREL ZIEGLER."

T he year 1925 did not begin auspiciously for the Ku Klux Klan in New Jersey—even in its Monmouth County stronghold. Reverend George H. Lawson was the cause of this. Lawson was a Monmouth County Klan Kludd (chaplain) who had publicly stated he was disillusioned with and leaving the organization and would run for Congress. The local *Freehold Transcript* newspaper derided Lawson's intentions, stating that "his sole purpose was to gain publicity for himself to get his candidacy for Congress before the people." The paper went on to report that the self-ordained evangelical preacher had borrowed money from his landlady, which he had yet to repay, and he was generally considered to be an unreliable person.[124]

The New Jersey press was apparently unaware of Lawson's sordid backstory. Born in London in 1864, he and his parents immigrated to Canada and then to the United States. Lawson did not stay put, however. At sixteen, he returned to England, where he joined the British army and served on garrison duty in Ireland and India. It appears he had time for recreational activities, as he was hospitalized for venereal disease and committed to an asylum before being medically discharged with the notation "manic" in 1886.[125]

After Lawson returned to America, he and his brother got involved in organizing baseball teams and leagues during the sport's professional infancy. Lawson, at times concealed by an alias, engaged in dubious, even dishonest business practices. His personal life was just as shady. On one occasion in the 1890s, he threatened to shoot his wife, one of six women he wed.[126]

After a stint as a door-to-door sewing machine salesman, Lawson became a vaudevillian, touring as "Professor Lawson, Hypnotist." While performing at a theater in Passaic, New Jersey, Lawson used the theater owner's wife as his assistant. Evidently, she assisted him offstage as well, as her husband subsequently caught the couple at Lawson's Manhattan apartment. Scheduled for another Passaic theater, Lawson failed to appear when he heard that his lover's husband was looking for him and had "a gun in his pocket."[127]

It seemed to occur to Lawson that a transition from vaudevillian to physician was the next logical step in his colorful career. The authorities in Connecticut did not concur. Charged by the state with practicing medicine without a license in 1910, he skipped out and began organizing a baseball league in Pennsylvania. Ironically, considering his future role with the Ku Klux Klan, Lawson, on this occasion and others, broke the color line and hired black baseball players for his proposed integrated league.[128]

In 1914, following the outbreak of World War I, Lawson moved to Boston, where he became a recruiter for the Canadian Royal Engineer regiment. He would, some years later, claim he had served at the front in France with the regiment. In fact, he never left Massachusetts. After the war, he dabbled in baseball once more before moving to Orange, New Jersey.[129]

Lawson's next reinvention was as an evangelical minister in Orange. Unwed at the moment, he advertised for a "prayer bride" in countrywide newspapers and chose Ella Weiber of Keyport, New Jersey, from his many replies. In September 1924, after a failed evangelism tour, Lawson and his bride went to Keyport and took over an abandoned Baptist chapel. This is when he began his relationship with the Monmouth County Klan. Considering his background, he was a natural for a leadership slot in the organization, although he undoubtably did not mention that he was ineligible for membership due to his foreign birth. In December, Lawson abruptly resigned from the Klan, claiming, with an uncharacteristic display of honesty and ethical outrage, that money from his collections had gone toward buying two new cars for Arthur Bell. Klansmen demonstrated outside his church in protest, and Lawson alleged the local Klan had threatened his life. To emphasize that he was ready to fight, he posed for a news photo holding a Bible and a revolver with a Klan hood on the table beside him.[130]

Following his disavowal of the Klan, Lawson ran unsuccessfully as an independent candidate for Congress, using the campaign motto "Kan the Klan. Vote for Lawson." Lawson moved to Matawan following his eviction from the Keyport church. There, he was involved in a domestic dispute—in

"Reverend" George H. Lawson and his "prayer bride," Ella Weiber, of Keyport, New Jersey. *From Library of Congress.*

which he threw and hit the town's police chief in the face with a plate—while inebriated. He was sentenced to thirty days in jail and, upon release, moved to Newark, where he worked as a painter until he met an anticlimactic end. In 1927, George H. Lawson fell off a ladder and died.[131]

Lawson's public antics did not appear to have an immediate impact on the appeal of the Klan in Monmouth County. In March 1925, Commissioner William F. Brighton of Avon and H.N. Benson of Asbury Park purchased the Radio Corporation of America property in Wall Township with a reputed $225,000 mortgage. The property, previously the Marconi Company's Belmar Station, was once the largest site in the Marconi wireless system and had been used to link New York and London. The property totaled 396 acres and contained "a thirty-eight-room hotel, two bungalows, four farms and farmhouses."

The new owners were rumored to be front men for the Ku Klux Klan. When asked by a reporter if that was the case, Commissioner Brighton replied that he was "not in a position to discuss that angle." In fact, the

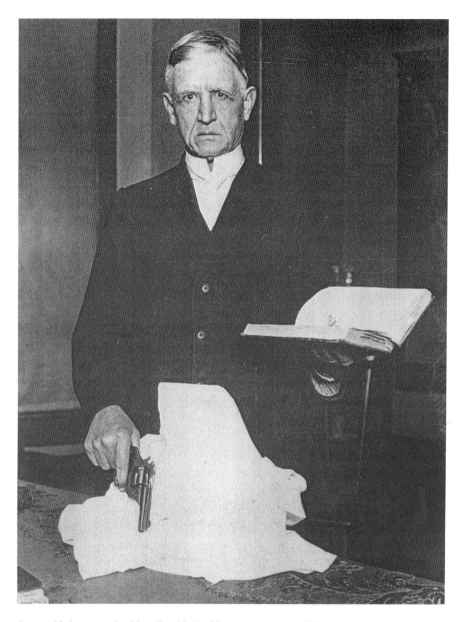

George H. Lawson after his split with the Klan, posing with a Bible, a revolver and a Klan hood. *From Library of Congress.*

actual owners of the property were members of the Point Pleasant and Asbury Park Klan chapters, incorporated as the Monmouth Pleasure Club. Arthur Bell, ever the performer, initially declared his intention to use the property as the base of a national Klan radio network, airing entertainment and Klan-approved news, although that never materialized.[132]

The next month, the national Klan suffered a major blow that also impacted the New Jersey Klan. In 1925, Indiana Grand Dragon "Steve" Stephenson was head of the most successful state branch of the entire Ku Klux Klan. Stephenson was a natural-born huckster and organizer who was adept at bragging about nonexistent prior accomplishments. He succeeded in

Indiana Grand Dragon David Curtis "Steve" Stephenson. *From Library of Congress.*

massively enlarging the Indiana Klan—an accomplishment that garnered him a rapid rise in the national organization and ensured the trust and confidence of Imperial Wizard Evans, who appointed him chief recruiter for seven midwestern states. Stephenson, whose ego matched his apparent oratorical skills, said, "I am a nobody from nowhere, really—but I've got the biggest brains."[133]

Stephenson was involved in Indiana state politics and was a confidante of Republican governor Edward L. Jackson, who was suspected of being a Klansman himself. Although espousing the usual Klan dogma, including a defense of "white Protestant womanhood," Stephenson was a heavy drinker and serial bigamist. Rumors of Stephenson's excesses, including locking ladies in hotel rooms and biting them repeatedly, were rampant but managed to stay hidden from the public.[134]

Stephenson's friendship with an Indiana state employee, Madge Oberholzer, raised the curtain on his sordid secret life. On March 15, 1925, during a "business" trip to Chicago, he abducted Oberholzer and confined her in his private train car. There, he drugged, sexually assaulted and tortured her. Oberholzer, feeling she was "ruined" by the experience, attempted suicide by taking mercury chloride. Rather than seek any help or medical attention for her, Stephenson dropped off the young woman at her mother's house, where she later died due to the poison combined with an infection. Before she died, Oberholzer was able to provide a statement to the police. Stephenson was arrested, charged with and convicted of second-degree murder.[135]

The Stephenson trial, which disclosed that Oberholzer's body was covered with bite marks, including a "significant" one on her breast, proved disastrous to the Klan. Indiana membership collapsed, and the negative impact was felt nationwide. Sentenced to life in prison and denied a requested pardon, while he was in prison Stephenson released documents revealing that many Indiana politicians, including the governor, were essentially on the Klan payroll.[136]

Meanwhile, back in New Jersey, there was Roscoe Carl Ziegler, a Methodist minister and World War I veteran with a wife and two children who was an up-and-coming Kleagle in Trenton. The twenty-eight-year-old clergyman was an excellent example of the native-born, white "real American" the Klan sought to glorify, so it was hardly a surprise that his star was on the rise. Nonetheless, a slight glitch arose. On July 4, 1925, Reverend Ziegler disappeared with $1,000 (more than $13,000 in 2016) of Klan money and his next-door neighbor, twenty-two-year-old Margaret "Peggy" Roberts.[137]

Peggy's furious fiancé, William Chamberlain, who worked for the *Trenton Times* newspaper, hired a private detective. The Jersey Klan, looking to recover its money, made its usual noise about vigilante law enforcement and sent out flyers to every Kleagle in the country to be on the lookout for the errant minister. The couple was eventually discovered in El Paso, Texas, where a photographer snapped a picture as Roscoe covered his face and Peggy smiled for the camera. Chamberlain traveled to Texas with his detective, apparently made a citizen's arrest of sorts and brought the couple back to New Jersey for prosecution under the Federal Mann Act—transporting a woman across state lines for "an immoral purpose." Ironically, Ms. Roberts was also liable for Mann Act prosecution as a participant in a conspiracy to violate the law.[138]

Roscoe had other problems as well. Arthur Bell wanted his $1,000 back, and he wanted compensation for $596.96 in expenses incurred during the pursuit, as he had hired private detectives in lieu of his promised Klan posse. On his return to New Jersey, Ziegler was arraigned for embezzlement in Red Bank and held in the Monmouth County jail with a $10,000 bail. He was released within twenty-four hours, after his parents repaid the Klan, and Bell dropped the charges. He and Peggy fled to his parents' home in Milford, Pennsylvania.

Back in Trenton, a reporter was interviewing Peggy's mother at her home on Edgemere Avenue when United States deputy marshal Woodbury B.

Runaway Kleagle Roscoe Carl Ziegler and Margaret "Peggy" Roberts in Texas. *From Joseph Bilby.*

Snowden showed up with a warrant for Peggy. When asked if she was at home, her mother responded, "You will find her at Milford, Pennsylvania, with that scoundrel Ziegler." Snowden visited the Ziegler home in Pennsylvania but could not find the elusive duo. State police were deployed along the Pennsylvania border to intercept Reverend Ziegler should he attempt to sneak back into New Jersey.[139]

By the end of August, Ziegler and Roberts voluntarily returned to New Jersey. They were arraigned separately in Newark on charges of conspiracy to violate the Mann Act and released on bail. According to press reports, Roscoe's wife, Marie, was going to divorce him, in an apparent gesture of magnanimity, to avoid charges against Peggy. She filed a divorce petition in Chancery Court in Trenton, while denying there was any "collusion" with her husband or others to dodge the Mann Act charges.[140]

In October, a federal grand jury in Trenton, after considering the case for three days, declined to indict the couple. By that time, Roscoe and Marie had reconciled, and Mrs. Ziegler said that she was "delighted" at the outcome. She continued with, "I am awfully glad. He has started working again and a thing like that hovering over him was a big shadow."[141]

The Zieglers later moved to either Virginia or Florida, where Roscoe was rumored to have resumed preaching as a Congregational minister. As is often the case, complications muddy the real story. According to the census of 1930, Ziegler was living with his parents in Pennsylvania and writing short stories. By 1940, he and his wife and children were living in Middletown, New York, and he described himself as a freelance writer with no income. By 1942, the family had moved to Paterson, New Jersey. When Roscoe Carl Ziegler died in 1958, he was buried where he was born: Milford, Pennsylvania. On the application for his veterans' grave marker, the box for religion was checked as "none."

In March 1925, amid the chaos, the Red Bank Business Men's Association decided to hold a "popularity contest" for local organizations. The voting was not strictly moderated, and ballots or "voting coupons" were available to customers in stores around the town. After the first three days of voting, the Ku Klux Klan was in the lead with 754 votes, followed by the fire department with 742. A myriad of other organizations was represented on the list, including the Eastern Star, Knights of Columbus, National Guard Cavalry Troop, police department, Children of Mary Sodality, the YMCA and the Young Women's Hebrew Association. Publication of those results apparently revolted anti-Klan forces, and the month-long contest ended with the fire department in first place with 100,286 votes, followed by the Klan with 76,845. The Knights of Columbus and the Ladies' Hebrew Society came in third and fourth, respectively. Red Bank was proving to be a mixed bag with growing anti-Klan leanings.[142]

There is no doubt that the Ziegler incident damaged the New Jersey Ku Klux Klan, especially on the heels of the Lawson and Stephenson coverage. Public perception also suffered from an eight-foot burning cross erected on Heller Parkway in Newark by alleged Klansmen who fled the scene as police arrived. The Ziegler incident may have been the initiating factor of a decline in the organization's actual membership numbers, although the difficulty in proving this lies in the fact that the actual membership numbers were never disclosed to the public. Arthur Bell's reaction was telling. Now the official King Kleagle of the state, he took to the offensive during the avalanche of unwelcome news.[143]

Bell attempted to soften the Klan's image with a Mother's Day rally in the Methodist "camp meeting" and vacation town of Ocean Grove. On May 11, 1925, an estimated eight thousand people, including "a large representation of Klan members from various parts of the state," attended the ceremony in the massive Great Ocean Grove Auditorium "under the auspices of the Women of the Ku Klux Klan, Knights of the Ku Klux Klan, American Krusaders, Junior Klansmen and the Tri-K-Klub of America." Bell and Leah conducted the day's services and were assisted by several ministers. It was hard to determine how many of the attendees were actual Klan members, as the audience was not robed. The King Kleagle credited the idea for the Mother's Day event to his flunky, Walter Tindall, who had been at the center of the bungled effort to remove Asbury Park's Mayor Clarence Hetrick in 1924.[144]

The Elkwood Park Klan Band performed on the stage "in full regalia," and Bell claimed in his opening remarks that "more mothers had heard from their sons throughout the state

Promotional advertisement for the 1925 Klan Mother's Day rally in Ocean Grove. *From Joseph Bilby.*

A period postcard view of the Ocean Grove auditorium, scene of the 1925 Mother's Day rally held by Arthur and Leah Bell. *From Joseph Bilby.*

than at any time in the last ten years" due to Mr. Tindall's efforts. Mrs. Bell followed her husband at the podium, claiming "moral education is the great need in America today, and the Ku Klux Klan is here to put the foundation in place." Mrs. Bell called for an "eight-hour day for mothers," saying that "father may get tired and will go into the next room and take a nap, but mother—did you ever see mother go to sleep when there is anything to do." She went on to credit her "Tri-K-Klub recently organized for junior girls" with teaching the young ladies that "there is something more in the world besides pleasure, and that is motherhood." She concluded with a call to pastors to "get together and promote pure womanhood."[145]

Bell returned to the podium and said, "I don't know how many Jews, Catholics or colored people there are in this audience today, but I don't believe there is one willing to fight against any organization that stands up for the principles of motherhood." A soloist crooned "Mother of Mine," and then the audience sang "The Old Rugged Cross" and filed out as the Klan Band played "Onward, Christian Soldiers."[146]

Although Methodist pastors and congregations provided a reliable and favorable audience for the Ku Klux Klan in New Jersey, the admiration of the Klan was not universal in that church. Methodist Episcopal bishop J.F. Berry of Philadelphia, whose diocese covered New Jersey, was decidedly not a Klan fan. Berry admonished candidates for the ministry about joining the

Above: The Ocean Grove auditorium today. *From Joseph Bilby.*

Right: Leah Bell holds forth at the 1925 Ocean Grove Mother's Day event. *From Joseph Bilby.*

organization, stating that it was not part of their job as pastors to become "public detectives" or "ferret out transgressors."[147]

Later in May, Bell advised the press that there would be a huge Klan gathering of as many as twenty-five thousand people from New Jersey, New York, Pennsylvania and Delaware on the Elkwood Park property. It was to be on May 23, complete with fireworks and a Klan baseball game between the "Long Branch Kavaliers and the Mercer County Klan." There was no follow-up report on how many attended the event.[148]

On the evening of May 31, Memorial Day, the Bell caravan pulled into the town of Lake Como, adjacent to Belmar. The King Kleagle spoke to a crowd inside and outside the Methodist church, using loudspeakers attached to car roofs to broadcast his message throughout the neighborhood. The church was crowded, but the total number of Klansmen and women, including Tri-K and Junior Klan members, was only around one hundred people, according to reporters.[149]

Bell asserted that "the Bible should be taught in our public schools. It should be taught as part of the curriculum. If the large band of aliens who come to our shores say, when we tell them that we teach the Bible in our schools, 'we don't like that' then the thing to do is load them on ships and send them back where they came from." He failed to mention that a "Bible Bill," providing for the enactment of his wishes and promoted by the Klan, had stalled in the New Jersey legislature in both 1924 and 1925.[150]

Bell went on to say, "Sooner or later America has got to meet the issue and decide whether she shall be Protestant or Catholic—whether the public or parochial school shall rule." He concluded on a conciliatory note, characterizing the Klan as a peaceful civic organization, saying, "The Ku Klux Klan is not going out with guns, swords or poisonous gas, but with a program of enlightenment, to accomplish this task."[151]

Farther north, in Hillsdale, Bergen County, the Rawson brothers took it upon themselves to "save" Protestant America as the increasing number of Catholics who had moved into the town planned to create a new parish. The local Klan had ordered Helen Riley, the widow of a county freeholder, not to sell land to the parish committee, but she metaphorically slapped their faces by donating it, and ground was broken for Saint John's Catholic Church on June 25, 1925.[152]

Pious local widow Teresa Murray initiated a campaign to establish a new parish, and fundraising events and money donated by her in-laws financed the construction. In a desperate effort to obstruct, several Klansmen in full regalia paid an evening visit to church committee activist John Buckley in nearby River Vale. They warned Buckley that unless he desisted, they would "run him out of town." Before slamming the front door in their hooded faces, Buckley responded, "You go right ahead and try it." A series of theatrical cross burnings ensued, including one near the Murray house that so traumatized her young son Henry that he recalled it vividly for the rest of his life. Nevertheless, the church was completed, and Buckley remained a resident of River Vale.[153]

By midsummer, Bell probably thought he was quite effective in recovering from the damaging national and local Klan publicity that had been so pervasive during the first half of the year. Two weeks later, however, bad news returned. Ocean County Kleagle Reverend Elmer Finger, pastor of the New Egypt Methodist Episcopal Church, and his friend, George A. Rawley, were charged with embezzling church funds. Finger claimed his accusers were "bootleggers, libertines and crooked politicians." The charges were dropped, much to Mr. Bell's relief.[154]

The Bells returned to the Great Ocean Grove Auditorium on July 19 to address another large crowd "almost entirely of Klan members or sympathizers" on the topic of "the flag, and the American home and the Bible." Again, the only people wearing robes were the Bells, so it was impossible to determine the number of actual Klan members in attendance. Bell likened the Ku Klux Klan to "a militant army for Christ" and compared the women of the Klan to "Betsey [sic] Ross in the early days of the nation" in their dedication to the country and its flag. Responding to calls for Klansmen to unmask, Bell answered, "The Ku Klux Klan will consider removing their masks when crooked politicians remove the masks from their souls and convents open their --- The last three words being utterly lost in the bedlam that broke loose," as the crowd cheered.[155]

As an example of the irony that seemed to stalk the New Jersey Klan, the Bells' performance at the auditorium was preceded by a Paul Robeson concert a day earlier. The *Asbury Park Press* wrote that Robeson "would give the same program of Negro music which caused such a big sensation in New York this spring." Grumbling Klansmen were unsuccessful in efforts to have Robeson's show cancelled.[156]

In August, the Bergen County branch of the Klan staged a parade that wended its way through Hackensack and other county municipalities. It drew thousands of spectators as well as hot dog vendors, fireworks and occasional roadside cross burnings. Around five thousand people were present, although how many were active Klansmen, as opposed to supporters and hecklers, is hard to determine. Among the spectators, "many Negroes lined the walks, taking in the proceedings with the nonchalance of skilled poker players." The Klan convoy was closely followed by a car driven by a Catholic priest who was caught in a traffic jam caused by the demonstration. The bizarre ruled here, as with many Klan events in New Jersey.[157]

Arthur Bell again took to the defensive as he dealt with a suicide that suggested Klan involvement. John Sampson of Port Monmouth, who in September 1925 shot himself in the heart while in a car at Sea Bright, left a vague note that blamed the Klan for his self-administered demise. He was allegedly a partner in a roadside stand business that was "said to be jointly owned by the Ku Klux Klan organizations of Keyport, Keansburg and Belford." Bell successfully stifled the story with a quick disavowal of Sampson's membership in the organization.[158]

In central New Jersey, the Klan staggered on, as did its penchant for exaggeration. Perhaps hoping to emulate and exceed the Bergen County event, the Somerset County Klan promised the public "a monster demonstration" for Labor Day. According to a spokesman, the day would feature a parade followed by a fair and carnival on local Klan property at the Owanamassee Country Club. The Klan claimed that "twenty-five thousand to fifty thousand Klansmen and women" from New York, Pennsylvania, Delaware, Maryland and New Jersey would attend the "Klonvocation" and march in a parade with accompanying brass bands. The crowd, including Klansmen and spectators, was estimated to total ten thousand people, only nine hundred of whom, "one-third of them women," participated in the parade. This was followed by the initiation of approximately four hundred people, or so the Klan claimed. The event reflected the August national march in Washington, D.C., in which less than half of the sixty thousand Klansmen predicted for the event showed up.[159]

In October 1925, the New Jersey Klan leadership reinforced attempts to broaden their appeal by portraying the organization as simply a patriotic movement dedicated to public welfare. The state organization had moved its headquarters to the local Klan-owned Monmouth Pleasure Club, the former Marconi Station in Wall Township, which was large enough to accommodate an evening "KKK Charity Circus" from October 19 to 24. Admittance was "open to all," presumably including African Americans, Catholics and Jews, who paid the fifty-cent admission fee. Access was convenient via a bus one could board on Fifth Avenue in Belmar. Traditional circus entertainment was interspersed with Klan patriotic demonstrations and a "Klan wedding."[160]

An advertisement for the Klan circus to be held on the Monmouth Pleasure Club property in Wall Township in October 1925. *From Joseph Bilby.*

The circus garnered the desired favorable reviews. A reporter depicted the opening night's events, which took place in a big top tent comically shaken by a wind that occasionally reached speeds of forty miles an hour, blowing in off the Shark River Inlet. The article described offerings by "15 groups of entertainers." These included "fancy riding by a dainty equestrienne," trapeze acts, an "equilibrist" who demonstrated "clever balancing of tables and chairs," vocal performances, a quintet of red-wigged, horse-riding clowns, jugglers and others. The journalist concluded his story by lauding the "lowly hot dog" and hot coffee served at a booth outside the tent. It was the best press the Klan had all year.[161]

The good fortune did not endure as violence in the following month brought unfavorable exposure. On November 3, Newark jeweler and Klansman William J. Clark got out of his car in front of his Hillside home, leaving his wife, Mrs. Priscilla Clark, and her mother, Mrs. Caroline Kent, in the vehicle. He walked around to the side door to open the garage from the inside. A few minutes later, Clark staggered out, his head covered with blood, and fell on the driveway. The women awoke Mrs. Clark's stepfather

Left: Klansman William J. Clark was hammered to death in Hillside in November 1925. *From Joseph Bilby*.

Right: Clark's widow, Priscilla, was initially detained as a material witness, allegedly on the advice of the Klan. She was later released. *From Joseph Bilby*.

and called a doctor and the police, who found a bloodstained five-pound mason's hammer on the floor of the garage. Clark said he did not know who hit him, and then he died.[162]

A group of forty Klansmen and women held funeral rites, including burning a cross, at Clark's burial, then vowed to launch an investigation, which, as usual, produced nothing. Mrs. Clark was arrested as a material witness but was released on bail. Klan members claimed to the press, without foundation, that their detective work had been responsible for the temporary detention of Mrs. Clark. Police later arrested Joseph Cowan, an ironworker who was a friend of Clark's and a reputed Klansman. He, however, had abandoned his wife and child in New York and allegedly asked Mrs. Clark to run away with him to Florida. Charged with murder, Cowan was eventually acquitted in March 1926, after a well-publicized trial. The murder was never solved.[163]

Klan conflict continued, even in Monmouth County. In October, the Red Bank Klavern, one of the strongest in Monmouth County, petitioned Mayor William H.R. White for a November 11 Armistice Day parade

The Red Bank Klan, complete with patriotic float, marches down East Front Street in the town's Armistice Day parade on November 11, 1925. *From Dorn's Classic Images.*

permit. The mayor denied the application but was overruled by his borough council. Widespread public disapproval included the Lions Club, which demanded that "all organizations and all citizens be invited to participate." As expected, the town's chapter of the Rainbow Division World War Veterans protested Klan involvement as well. The Red Bank National Guard unit had served as the 42nd Rainbow Division's 165th Ambulance Company during the war. The veterans noted that "the only time soldiers wore masks was when they had to do so to protect themselves against poison gas." In the end, the Klan was allowed to march, but the effect was offset by participation of other groups.[164]

In 1926, Arthur Hornbui Bell would officially be designated the first Ku Klux Klan Grand Dragon of New Jersey and would lead New Jersey Klansmen in another national march in Washington, D.C. The giant parade that fall would be his last hurrah.

CHAPTER 6

"THE KLAN MAY HAVE THOUSANDS OF VOTES, AS IT STATES, BUT I CANNOT ALLOW ANY BODY OF CITIZENS TO DICTATE TO ME."

The grand ceremony accentuated Arthur Hornbui Bell's public role in growing the Ku Klux Klan and its influence along a somewhat rocky road in New Jersey. On March 17, 1926, at Elkwood Park in Long Branch, Bell was officially "elevated to the rank of grand dragon of the realm of New Jersey." The honors were bestowed by Imperial Klazik H.K. Ramsey, second in command to Imperial Wizard Hiram Evans. Bell was also presented with an official charter for the realm by Ramsey.[165]

Although Bell has usually been considered the New Jersey grand dragon from 1922 to 1940, that was not the case, as he didn't receive the title until 1926. The one thousand Klansmen present at the ceremony burned a cross at midnight in celebration. Although the local Klan members who had owned Elkwood Park had sold the property, apparently due to inability to continue paying the mortgage, it was still in use for Klan purposes, likely by lease from the new owners.

Gifts bestowed on Bell included a "Grand Dragon's banner" from Bergenfield Klan No. 58, with a stand for the banner from Ridgewood Klan No. 72. In his first official act, the Grand Dragon appointed three unnamed "Great Titans" as his subordinates to rule the newly created three Klan provinces of the state. Internal dissension marred the claim of Bell and his adherents that his elevation met with unanimous approval across the Klaverns of the state.[166]

Some mild internal controversy may have stirred when Klan ladies extended an invitation to Margaret Sanger to speak at the Wall Township property. While later lauded as a pioneer champion of women's health, at the time Sanger's birth control advocacy carried mixed messages. She was frequently vilified by conservatives as a member of the urban "elites" who were sullying the United States' pristine character by encouraging promiscuity with such radical notions as easy access to birth control. Sanger's advocacy was promoted by others as a possible remedy for a perceived population crisis facing "real Americans" with the growing immigrant and ethnic communities and their rising birth rate in contrast to a stagnant "native" (white Protestant) demographic.

Margaret Sanger spoke to a Klan women's gathering at the New Jersey headquarters in Wall Township in May 1926. *From Joseph Bilby*.

Where Sanger stood on this issue is debated to this day. While there is no evidence that she held membership in the Klan, she embraced some of the tenets of the eugenics movement, including ideas on who should and should not reproduce. These beliefs were quite common at the time, even in progressive and academic circles. One prominent eugenicist told a congressional committee, "We want to prevent the deterioration of the American people due to the immigration of inferior human stock." This belief aligned with the Klan's views on the subject.[167]

In her autobiography, Sanger detailed her journey in May 1926, to an almost comical degree. As she headed to the Klan venue, it was clear she had no idea where she was. She had received a letter telling her to get off the train at the Belmar station and walk several blocks one way and several blocks in another direction to a certain restaurant and wait ten minutes. After ten minutes, she entered a car in front of the restaurant, which then took a circuitous route around and out of town and down a road before finally driving down a dirt lane to a barn-like building overlooking a body of water—the Klan headquarters on the Monmouth Pleasure Club property. After waiting for hours in the parked car, observing Klanswomen arrive, Sanger entered the venue. Although she was happy with her reception, she recalled that it was one of the "weirdest experiences" she had ever had. The secret meeting was not mentioned in the local press or any other newspaper. The event would likely have been lost to history had not Sanger recorded her escapade in her memoirs.[168]

The elevation of Bell to Grand Dragon managed to eliminate or minimize any repercussions and dissension from the Sanger talk. However, real trouble soon followed when Mrs. Carol C. Miller of Atlantic City, a former female Kleagle charged with recruiting women for the Klan, issued a statement claiming that two hundred women in the Atlantic and Cape May County chapter had resigned and joined a rival organization she alleged she was creating called "the Klina."[169]

Miller claimed that "mismanagement is rampant today in the Ku Klux Klan." She also asserted, although without evidence, that it was "the easiest thing in the world to join the order. Some of the most notorious of Atlantic City's bootleggers are members." Miller had been summoned to appear before Klan judges in November 1925, on charges brought by Leah Bell of "misconduct, frequenting cabarets and [mis]appropriating funds," so she had a personal axe to grind. Miller, claiming the charges against her were false, resigned and said that "more than one hundred fifty friends followed her." She asserted that "the present Klan regime in New Jersey is controlled by the Bell family and is rapidly causing the disintegration of both men's and women's organizations."[170]

The Klan had apparently learned nothing from the disastrous Perth Amboy riot of 1923. They requested a permit to hold a parade in, of all places, Jersey City—a municipality with a large, vocal and politically powerful immigrant and Catholic population. The applicant was Arthur Bell's associate Reverend Alton Milford Young of Belmar, the ostensible Grand Klokard of the New Jersey Klan, who inflated the anticipated participants to as many as thirty thousand Klansmen and Klanswomen. Perhaps fortunately for the Klan, Irish Catholic Democratic mayor and iconic Hudson County political boss Frank Hague denied the application, stating that such an event would lead to "rioting and lawlessness." Hague was not alone in his rejection of Klan parades, of course, as the mayors of Atlantic City and Trenton had previously denied march permits to the organization, and the mayor of Philadelphia declined a similar request for Klan participation in the city's 1926 sesquicentennial celebrations.[171]

Grand Dragon Bell soon turned on the charm again as he advertised a June 13 "Great Revival Service" at the Wall Township property. It would be the first in a series of Sunday services, each featuring a "prominent minister" and a "Klan band, choir and orchestra" that would offer a "sacred concert."

Great Revival Services

EVERYBODY WELCOME

KU KLUX KLAN

Revival Services

GRAND OPENING

Sunday, June 13, 3 P. M. Rain or Shine

For All Men, Women and Children, Regardless of
Race, Color or Creed.

A Prominent Minister Will Deliver the Sermon.

Klan Choir, Band and Orchestra Will Offer a Sacred Concert.

KLAN HAVEN

Formerly Marconi Wireless Station

RIVER ROAD, BELMAR, N. J.

TO THE PUBLIC:

This Sunday will mark the opening of a regular Sunday afternoon revival service under the auspices of the Klans. Each Sunday afternoon a different minister will deliver the Word of God and many prominent ministers have been booked for these Sunday afternoon services. Everyone is invited. These are not Klan lectures, but religious services for the spreading of God's Holy Word. The opening Sunday, June 13th, will see hundreds present from Hudson and Essex Counties and elsewhere and you are cordially invited to join with us in these services every Sunday afternoon at 3 o'clock.   ARTHUR H. BELL,
Grand Dragon, Realm of N. J.

An advertisement for the revival meeting scheduled for the Monmouth Pleasure Club property in Wall Township in June 1926. *From Joseph Bilby.*

Most telling was the notice that "everybody" was invited, including "all men, women and children, regardless of race, color or creed." There are no attendance records for the services.[172]

Not everyone was enthralled by the Klan's religious relationships, and a July appearance of hooded and robed members of the Asbury Park Klavern at a Methodist church in Glendola, not far from the Klan property in Wall, was disrupted by what was described as a "tear gas bomb" but was more likely an amateur "stink bomb." The homemade device "was placed outside a window in such a position that the breeze carried the offensive fumes to the noses of those in the congregation." A car with Middlesex County license plates was observed leaving the scene.[173]

Discord in New Jersey and friction elsewhere could not halt planning for the year's highlight, a national convocation. On September 13, 1926, a massive march of Klan realms from around the country was held in Washington, D.C. The event was intended to replicate the prior year's parade and encourage Klan members countrywide. As Grand Dragon Bell led the New Jersey delegation down Pennsylvania Avenue, an observer noted

The national Ku Klux Klan parade in Washington, D.C., on September 13, 1926. *From Library of Congress.*

that the state "had one of the largest delegations, and, although every county was represented, most of the marchers, including nearly as many women as men," were from "the central part of the state," in other words, the Klan base from Somerset to Ocean Counties. The Paterson Klan, certainly not the most popular, exhibited a float carrying "'Miss One Hundred Percent

Left: New Jersey's "Miss 100 percent America" photographed at New Jersey Klan headquarters at the Monmouth Pleasure Club in Wall Township. *From InfoAge Science History Learning Center and Museum*.

Opposite: Republican assemblyman Basil Bruno of Long Branch introduced the Klan's "Bibles in Schools" legislation and then ran unsuccessfully for Monmouth County sheriff. *From Joseph Bilby*.

America,' who held an open Bible and her court." Observers estimated the number of marchers as about half of the previous year and perceived the reduction as a sign of a troubled Klan.[174]

As elections approached, the New Jersey Klan turned its attention to politics. The results in some local races were disappointing for them. Republican assemblyman Basil Bruno of Long Branch, who had introduced the Klan's "Bibles in Schools" legislation, despite a Klan "Fiery Summons" calling out the faithful to vote for him, lost his bid for Monmouth County sheriff in an overwhelming defeat. The "Summons" bore a picture of Bruno and a pledge by him to "wipe out the roadhouse evils that exist in our country."[175]

Successful Republican candidates won with far smaller margins than in prior years. Why Bruno, a pharmacist born to Italian immigrants in Long Branch in 1887, would espouse a Klan goal remains a mystery. Perhaps he was influenced by his membership in the Methodist church and the anti-immigrant Junior Order of United American Mechanics. The JOUAM

was intimately connected with the Klan and often participated in Klan presentations of flags and Bibles. On one occasion, the Klan, allegedly competing with other patriotic organizations, won a "popularity contest" at a JOUAM meeting and in turn presented the chapter with a flag and an effusion of rhetoric.[176]

Bruno was also, according to a brief newspaper biography, "very active in church and fraternal organizations." An analysis of his electoral defeat opined that "there was a time when it was taken for granted that liaison with Klan leaders meant so many votes, but Tuesday's election turned this assumption topsy-turvy and showed, in Bruno's case, that the reverse obtains." Evidence suggests similar results countrywide.[177]

The Klan varied its political affiliations by supporting Democrats in the South and Republicans in the North. In Indiana, for example, Grand Dragon Stephenson's buddy, Republican governor Edward Jackson, was widely considered to be a Klan member. In Alabama, David Bibb Graves, the first governor to serve two four-year terms, was a Democrat. He was also said to be the Exalted Cyclops of the Ku Klux Klan.

The New Jersey political environment was complicated. Although local Republican officials in Klan strongholds such as Monmouth County, or in immigrant-fearing regions such as Bergen County, often allied themselves with the Klan, state Republican leaders did not. After the national Klan labeled moderate Republican senator Walter Edge a "reactionary" in 1923, the New Jersey Klan opposed him in the next year's primary with a claim that Edge lacked enthusiasm for prohibition. On the other hand, Senator James T. Heflin of Alabama got a Klan endorsement as a "progressive." A probable Klansman, he was responsible for promoting legislation intended to prevent African Americans from voting in his state, segregating public transit in Washington, D.C., and promising to ban the immigration of Catholics. This goes to show that the meaning of political labels over the years has often been fluid, shifting to attract a group or facilitate a desired outcome without concern for consistency.[178]

The marginal political influence of the Klan in New Jersey continued its downward spiral in 1927. Bergen County prosecutor A.C. Hart vowed to prosecute any Klan vigilantes should they act against local music shop owner Lester Schenck for his alleged affair with Mrs. Madeline Horner. After a "man in a robe" told Schenck to "get out of town within forty-eight hours," Hart assigned two police officers to guard Schenck's store and promised to "proceed against anyone" who took the law into their own hands.[179]

Two-time Republican New Jersey governor and senator Walter "Wally" Edge was opposed in the party primary by the Klan as a "reactionary" due to his lack of enthusiasm for prohibition. *From Joseph Bilby.*

Religious support also waned that year. Although in March 1927 a visit by two hundred Klansmen and women to the Netherwood Reformed Church in Plainfield was well received, in June a reception at the Central Methodist Episcopal Church in Point Pleasant was hardly warm. The church board expected one hundred male and female Klan members to respond to their invitation, but only thirty to forty showed up "carrying their regalia in small bags." They were advised by the pastor, Reverend Robert Anderson, that, on orders from "higher up," he could not allow a Klan representative to address his congregation. After arguing the point to no avail, the Klan members left in a huff and attended services at the Glendola Methodist Church.[180]

The Easter Sunrise Service in Somerset County became the most notable New Jersey Klan event of the year. Bugles blew loud and clear at four o'clock that morning, April 17, in Basking Ridge, Bernardsville, Liberty Corner, Millington, Far Hills, Bedminster and Peapack-Gladstone. In response, "a large majority of the population in these communities rubbed the sleep from their eyes and, hastily donning their Easter clothes, repaired to the Ridge center."[181]

In addition to locals who congregated at the center, cars from California, Connecticut, Texas, Florida, Delaware, Pennsylvania and New York, as well as elsewhere in New Jersey, had begun arriving the previous day and into the night. A reporter noted that there were about 3,500 automobiles parked along local highways and byways when their occupants stepped out, hooded and robed and ready to march. An outdoor breakfast was served to approximately four thousand Klan members, though the Klan had predicted attendance of twenty thousand. Then a lengthy line of men and women "began their pilgrimage to the Sunrise Service at Sunset Hill, about a half mile away"[182]

A journalist estimated that the marchers were joined by "several thousands more in civilian attire, which, with those who observed the demonstration, would make the total well on toward ten or twelve thousand people." One viewer noted that it took twenty-three minutes for the parade to pass a given point on the route. On arrival at Sunset Hill, the Klansmen were "serenaded by the Stirling male quartet and other musical organizations." An ambulance with a doctor and nurse on standby quickly aided "two women who became hysterical at the meeting."[183]

Imperial Wizard Hiram Wesley Evans, in the state as part of a national tour to revive his declining organization, addressed the crowd and was followed at the podium by Grand Dragon Bell and then Leah Bell. She, too, had a grand new title and was now known as the "Excellent Commander of the Realm of New Jersey." Following the speeches, a collection netting $1,064 was taken for Bishop Janes Methodist Episcopal Church in Basking Ridge. After the ceremonies ended at 7:30 a.m., the crowd jammed the roads, taking two hours for the last cars to clear the area.[184]

Evans continued to Jersey City to appear before a crowd of four thousand at the National Guard's Fourth Regiment Armory, which had been leased for the evening. As has been noted, Catholic- and immigrant-heavy Jersey City was not an ideal location for a Klan presentation, and Evans's safety in the venue was secured by a squad of policemen. His speech, "On Christianity, America and the Klan," was "accompanied by a wonderful program of special music" and was broadcast by the radio station WAAT, where wires that had been cut in five places in protest had been fixed by hasty repairs before the broadcast.

The Imperial Wizard slammed New York governor Al Smith, the Catholic son of Irish and Italian immigrants, whose rising political star made him a

The New Jersey Klan event of 1927 was the Easter Sunday Sunrise Service held in Somerset County on April 17. These Klansmen are marching to the venue. *From Joseph Bilby.*

likely presidential candidate in 1928. A surprised reporter spotted Stephen Newson, a single African American, in the crowd. When the reporter asked the "butler in a Jersey City home" why he was there, Newson replied that he "felt that the Klan's activities were directed not against the Negroes, but against the Catholics."[185]

Smith's potential candidacy was regarded as fuel to revitalize the Klan and get beyond its recent scandals. As the year ended, the organization began to ramp up its campaign against the New York governor. In New Jersey, Arthur and Leah Bell announced that they were launching a fundraising drive to oppose Smith, but their efforts were distracted by a growing internal dispute over the ownership of the Monmouth Pleasure Club property. This simmering feud would continue into 1928 and escalate into a public relations disaster.

The year 1928 began with a distraction, however, as members of the Asbury Park Reformed Church were angry that an invitation to a Klan

Imperial Wizard Evans spoke at the Easter ceremony as part of his tour intended to reverse declining enrollment in the Klan. *From Joseph Bilby.*

The last venue of Evans's New Jersey tour, the Jersey City Armory. *From Joseph Bilby.*

meeting in Freehold had been mailed using church-marked envelopes. The former church secretary, a Klansman and no longer a parishioner, had apparently decided to use church stationery he already had as a budgetary consideration. The letter included an announcement that there would be a one-dollar admission fee to the meeting—a further indication that the local Klan may have fallen upon fiscally challenging times.[186]

Adding insult to the injury of dismal finances, the Klan's hood and sheet regalia was ridiculed in a sketch in the *Asbury Park Press*. The cartoon, entitled "Household Hints—That Discarded K.K.K. Regalia," suggested that a Klansman who left the order could find several uses for his hood, from acting as a lampshade to decorating fireplace andirons or protecting him from summer mosquito bites. There was more than a hint of mockery in the suggestions.[187]

This *Asbury Park Press* cartoon from early 1928 is symbolic of the Klan's increasing lack of relevance, even in its Monmouth County stronghold. *From Joseph Bilby.*

Arthur Bell made one of the biggest mistakes of his career in April 1928, when he assumed that the Republican Party desired, and would be grateful for, Klan support for Herbert Hoover as president as well as for down-ticket candidates. He rented a room at the Robert Treat Hotel in Newark, a popular political watering hole, and announced that he was inviting Republican primary candidates to appear on the afternoon of April 22. Bell explained that he and four members of his "political intelligence committee" would be questioning the candidates on their "Americanism," intimating that Klan support would be awarded to those who answered satisfactorily. None of the candidates showed up, and a journalist noted that even the usual political operatives who hung around the hotel were notably absent.[188]

The response was rapid. When asked why he did not attend, United States senator Hamilton Kean, member of a famous New Jersey political family and a well-regarded Republican, stated, "I am not a member of the Ku Klux Klan, and never had anything to do with it. Why should I attend? The Klan may have thousands of votes, as it states, but I cannot allow any body of citizens to dictate to me." State Senator Morgan Larson, who was running for governor, admitted he had received an invitation but said he "did not want to discuss it." Bell declined to discuss it as well, but he must have been humiliated by the outcome.[189]

After this fiasco, Grand Dragon Bell avoided politics for a while. However, when a senator from Alabama came to New Jersey that summer and made a series of presentations that touted the Klan and targeted Al Smith and Catholics, the work was perceived as having been done under the aegis of Bell's New Jersey Realm.

Senator James Thomas Heflin, widely known as "Cotton Tom," was born in Alabama in 1869 and became one of the most "colorful" politicians in this tumultuous era. Heflin, an attorney and advocate of convict leasing, helped draft the 1901 Constitution of Alabama. While doing so, he claimed that God intended African Americans to be "servants of the white man." After Heflin was elected to Congress, he was an unabashed foe of women's suffrage. He displayed his backward vision by suggesting that a fellow Alabama congressman in favor of votes for women "wear a bonnet and dress." Heflin's uncle Robert Stell Heflin was, ironically, a Unionist during the Civil War and served as a Republican congressman during Reconstruction. He was the first southerner to deliver the annual Memorial Day observance at Gettysburg in 1913.[190]

In 1904, after campaigning to segregate seating on Washington, D.C. public transportation, Congressman Heflin shot and wounded a black

Right: The Robert Treat Hotel in Newark in the 1920s. Arthur Bell rented a room in this political watering hole in April 1928. He summoned politicians to appear and be tested on their "Americanism." None showed up. *From Joseph Bilby.*

Below: United States senator Hamilton Kean refused to attend Bell's inquisition and said, "I am not a member of the Ku Klux Klan, and never had anything to do with it. Why should I attend?" *From Joseph Bilby.*

Alabama senator James Thomas "Cotton Tom" Heflin toured New Jersey as a Klan front man attacking Democratic presidential candidate Alfred Smith. *From Joseph Bilby.*

man who confronted him on a streetcar. Charged with assault, Heflin claimed self-defense. Although the charges were dismissed, Heflin ended up paying the man's hospital bill. The case did not prove an impediment to his election to the Senate. If not an actual Ku Klux Klan member, Heflin was a strong sympathizer, and throughout the 1920s, he added Catholics, Jews and immigrants to his list of perceived enemies.[191]

In March 1928, Senator Heflin received a package containing a violin from an anonymous donor. The senator, who was more than a little paranoid, asked postal inspectors to examine the violin for poison or germs and to find out who sent it to him, as Catholic agents were out to murder him.[192]

Heflin's anti-Catholic antipathies proved stronger than his Democratic Party membership, as he strongly opposed the presidential candidacy of Al Smith. He traveled to New Jersey in July 1928 to address Ku Klux Klan chapters in Woodbridge, Rutherford and Long Branch and spoke out against Smith's candidacy while also railing on about his other obsessions.

During an appearance before a crowd of four hundred in Woodbridge, the Alabama senator announced that he was proposing legislation to ban the entry of Catholics into the country for five years. In Rutherford, a smaller gathering of the Albert Pike Klan No. 2 and their guests paid twenty-five cents a head to hear him rant. He charged that "they" had "tried to flood this country with Catholics through the immigration gates and I am glad I had something to do to stop that flood," referring to his, and the Klan's, support of the restrictive Immigration Act of 1924.[193]

Heflin attracted his largest audience in Long Branch. He spoke at Elkwood Park, where one thousand people were reportedly in the crowd, including "more than a hundred armed guards" of the Klan's "Kavaliers" to keep the senator safe from imagined Catholic agents. Calling for even more restrictions on immigration, Heflin predicted that "the day is coming when every Protestant in the United States will thank God that there is a Klan. It is the bulwark of the nation."[194]

That night, Senator Heflin stayed at the Monterrey Hotel in Asbury Park. The senator was a hefty fellow, and a couple of his bed slats broke. When a hotel representative and a carpenter arrived to fix the bed, Heflin refused to let them in before getting their physical description from management. Stirred by his personal demons, Heflin called down to the desk clerk to explain that he feared Catholics coming to kill him.[195]

After his anti–Al Smith tour, Senator Heflin was denied re-nomination by the Alabama Democratic Party.[196]

Although Heflin denied that he had been compensated by the Ku Klux Klan for his New Jersey trip, a letter from a leader of the "Women of the Ku Klux Klan" in Arkansas specified that his per-lecture honorarium was $125 ($1,781 in 2016). This led some to believe that Leah Bell had conducted business with the senator to provide cover for Arthur.[197]

A decade later, former New Jersey Republican congressman and governor Harold Hoffman was generous when he reflected on Heflin's state tour, saying, "I always thought that Heflin had his tongue in his cheek when he made those attacks; that he had found it politically and financially profitable to become the Senate champion of the K.K.K." Hoffman joked that "Frederick William Wile, the columnist, made him [Heflin] the basis of his immortal crack. 'An empty taxicab drew up to the Senate wing of the Capitol and Tom Heflin got out.'"[198]

On August 25, 1928, Democratic political boss Frank Hague and New Jersey governor A. Harry Moore held a massive political rally on behalf of Governor Al Smith at the Sea Girt National Guard Camp. The crowd of an estimated eighty thousand enthusiastic New Jersey Democrats cheered the candidate and sang his campaign song, "The Sidewalks of New York." Just up the road in Ocean Grove, evangelist Billy Sunday preached to the camp meeting crowd at the auditorium where the Bells had previously held forth. Although there is no evidence that Sunday was a Klansman, many of his beliefs coincided with those of the Klan. At Ocean Grove, Sunday railed against "radicals" and modernity and attacked Smith, condemning him as "a Tammanyite, a Catholic and a wet," as well as an ambassador of "the forces of hell."[199]

As the campaign heated up, so did the Jersey Klan. Arthur Bell returned to the limelight in September, making appearances in all twenty-one New Jersey counties at public events "to voice the Klan's sentiments concerning Governor Smith and his candidacy." At one of these events, reportedly attended by one thousand people and ironically on a field leased from "a Jewish realtor," Bell ranted about Smith being a "menace" to America because his Catholicism made him "an individual subservient to the hierarchy of Rome." Bell went on to equate the Democratic presidential candidate with Benedict Arnold before bewilderingly contradicting himself, stating that "the Klan as an organization is not in politics. We do not stoop that low." The Grand Dragon concluded by asserting, equally irrationally, that the Klan was not opposed to Smith because he was a Democrat or a Catholic, but because he was "not fit spiritually, mentally or morally for the high office to which he aspires."[200]

A theoretical argument could be made that there was a Catholic belief in intolerance based on the "error has no rights" philosophy espoused by Pope Pius IX. The pope had advocated that in a Catholic-majority country, Catholic views should dominate government, but it is doubtful that Al Smith, or for that matter any American Catholics, had a sincere belief in implementing that theory in the United States. It is also doubtful that vaudevillian Arthur Bell was specifically aware of it.[201]

On October 28, as election day approached, Bell held another rally in Neptune, attracting a crowd of five hundred. Confusion spread rapidly. The guest speakers were advertised in advance as being "Major Ruestettler of Brooklyn and Mrs. Piper of Newark," representatives of the Republican National Committee, but that body denied any such association. Even more bizarre, the two people who showed up to speak at the event identified themselves as Reverend Allen of Washington, D.C., and Reverend Cookson of Wisconsin, despite a reporter who overheard a Klan guard at the rally whisper to another that "no names are to be

The New Jersey governor's summer "cottage" at the National Guard camp in Sea Girt—site of the Al Smith rally in 1928. *From Joseph Bilby.*

Governor A. Harry Moore, Catherine Smith, Governor Al Smith and Jennie Moore at the Sea Girt rally in 1928. *From National Guard Militia Museum of New Jersey.*

Evangelist Billy Sunday preached against Al Smith in Ocean Grove while the Smith rally was staged a few miles to the south in Sea Girt. *From Joseph Bilby.*

Alma White attacked Al Smith repeatedly in the pages of her *Good Citizen* newsletter. *From Wikimedia Commons.*

mentioned here tonight." The Grand Dragon claimed he had been out of state and was unaware of the speakers' identities. All three mounted an "auto truck used as a rostrum" and proceeded to give anti-Smith rants, one of which contrasted the Democratic candidate unfavorably with Herbert Hoover, who was described as a "man of God."[202]

Al Smith brought the scrambled event to national attention when he referred to it in a speech in Baltimore as evidence of collusion between the Republican National Committee and the Ku Klux Klan. Both Bell and the Republicans denied the assertion vehemently.[203]

In the election, held on November 6, Hoover won forty states, including New Jersey. In a rather peculiar incident on the night before the election, a number of fliers stating that "the Klan wants you to vote for Hoover" appeared in "Newark's Third Ward, usually Republican and with a strong colored and Jewish vote." Both parties denied any knowledge of the source of the leaflets. There was little doubt that Smith's Catholicism, immigrant roots and New York accent, along with his opposition to prohibition and association with the Democratic Tammany Hall machine, were factors in his defeat. The apparent flourishing state of the economy gave Hoover a significant boost as well. The ardent anti-Catholicism of the 1928 campaign cast a cloud of doubt over the electability of a Catholic president that lasted until John F. Kennedy's victory in 1960.[204]

Grand Dragon Bell took credit for Hoover winning the state. He claimed his statewide speaking tour provided the margin of victory in New Jersey. Any self-assumed glory was short-lived as the Jersey Klan nosedived into a self-destructive spiral. A struggle over ownership of the Monmouth Pleasure Club property began in state and federal courts, while rumors of personal indiscretion haunted the Grand Dragon.

CHAPTER 7

"IT'S A GOOD FICTION STORY. I LIKE GOOD FICTION STORIES."

The week-long circus on the palatial grounds of the Monmouth Pleasure Club in Wall Township, New Jersey, beginning October 19, 1925, would prove to be perhaps the premier Klan event in the shore area since the Long Branch Klonklave. Event organizers noted that the show consisted of "some of the best circus acts in the business," including the Clark Brothers, a "sensational" aerial team, and Victory, the "wonder pony," which amazed the crowds with its ability to add, subtract and multiply.[205]

An exuberant reporter covering the October festivities for the *Asbury Park Press* noted that the circus "provided its many thrills for both the young and old in attendance." The evening concluded with a midnight wedding, which provided a memorable finish to an event attended by some two thousand revelers.[206]

However, undercutting the carnival jollity was a display of the sinister bigotry and intolerance of the Klan. The bride and groom, as well as other members of the wedding party, were garbed in the ghostly robes of the Ku Klux Klan. The ceremony, during which the couple were never identified, was officiated by Grand Dragon Arthur Bell, who presided over what he imagined to be a little empire on the banks of the Shark River Inlet. Bell incorrectly believed that his leadership had lifted the Klan onto a rising tide that would never crest.

Many events, in addition to the circus, were offered at the Klan compound. After its purchase in 1925, the Monmouth Pleasure Club Association published a promotional brochure that described the land in lush, idyllic tones as a sprawling tract with "an unobstructed view of river and sea." The grounds were dominated by a stately hotel, which was constructed for the Marconi Belmar Receiving Station. It had originally functioned as a housing headquarters for staff at the former international communication center. The red brick edifice with a tiled roof was described by its promoters as "a beautiful building, 200 feet long, facing the highway with a broad piazza extending across the entire front." The imposing building, with its forty-five bedrooms, large dining room and well-appointed lobby, possessed all the "necessary equipment for the operation of a high-class hotel," according to the *Asbury Park Press*. Indeed, its promoters boasted that "social affairs, balls, dinners and receptions, music and other attractions will lead many a tourist to spend a few days here."[207]

The surrounding grounds were no less impressive. The property, with its majestic view of the Shark River Inlet, boasted "tennis courts, ball diamonds and provision for other amusements, such as fairs and carnivals or athletic meets." Building upon the existing amenities, the Pleasure Club's plans envisioned a luxurious resort mecca. A supplemental concept involved dividing the vast expanse of remaining undeveloped land into building lots for homes and businesses that would be sold to its members, creating "a community of both permanent and summer residents near the sea that shall be entirely free from undesirable elements of every nature." Individual lot sales contracts forbid the buyer from selling to another person without Pleasure Club approval of the sale for twenty years.[208]

The exclusivity of its membership tore the mask off this self-styled utopian community, revealing the insidiousness of its true nature. As the *Asbury Park Press* noted, the Monmouth Pleasure Club's intention was clearly to provide a playground for the "spectral legions" of the Klan, whose "literature makes it plain that only members of the Ku Klux Klan, American Krusaders, Junior Klansmen and Tri-K-Klub will be permitted to use the hotel and other improvements." These deed restrictions were not unusual for the era, and clauses barring sale or occupancy to black people (other than live-in maids) and others—typically Italians—were still common in the 1920s.[209]

The Pleasure Club outlined its membership requirements more discreetly, vaguely noting, "Membership in this organization can only be by invitation of one who is already a member, and if the applicant is found to measure up to the standards required, he or she may be elected, provided the constitution and by-laws of the Association are subscribed to by the candidate."[210]

A questionnaire for potential Klan members was quite transparent. The introduction noted, "We have been requested by one of your personal friends to get in touch with you and inform you of this organization." The letter urged its recipients to fill out the form "without delay" and return it in an enclosed, stamped envelope. The questions began innocuously, with queries about age, occupation and similar topics. The inquiries quickly became more pointed, including "Are you a Gentile or Jew?" and "Do you believe in White Supremacy?"[211]

Indeed, it was no secret that the Klan's exclusionary ideals would be implemented at its new headquarters or that the Monmouth Pleasure Club was a business front for the group or at least its local membership. On March 14, 1925, the *Asbury Park Press* reported on the sale of the 396-acre tract to Mr. Brighton and Mr. Benson with a front-page headline blaring, "Purchase of Big Marconi Tract for Klan Reported." The article stated that "according to those in the know," the property was to be the future home of the Ku Klux Klan. The story went on to note, "It is reported that the Klan, which has adopted the name of the Monmouth Pleasure Club for business purposes, ultimately will occupy the hotel as a meeting place and that the Klan as a body or a Klan corporation will develop the property… establishing a Klan colony." When asked if the property was to be turned into a meeting place for the Klan, Brighton weakly responded that "he did not think so."[212]

Brighton's mild denial was clearly false, and the Klan quickly laid claim to its kingdom by the sea. By 1926, the resort was in a robust first stage of growth: "Already tent colonies have risen and a number of bungalows have been erected," a local newspaper noted. As promised, the property became the site of a dizzying whirlwind of social activities, including the week-long circus and a three-day July Fourth celebration in 1926. To promote the July event, it was announced that "an American flag will fly from a balloon during the celebration, and Klan officials have declared that this will be visible for twenty miles."[213]

The July festivities began with a grand ball and reception held on Saturday evening, July 3. On Sunday, all were invited to a "patriotic rally" featuring "state and national speakers," including Imperial Wizard Evans, who was scheduled to arrive "by aeroplane from Illinois." The schedule for that day included an important reminder that all members could wear their regalia or "may mingle with the crowd." Ever mindful of the need for anonymity, the reminder added in all capital letters, "IF YOU WEAR YOUR REGALIA, PUT YOUR VISOR DOWN AND KEEP IT DOWN." The extravaganza concluded on Monday with speeches, a band concert, a parade and the burning of the "Old Fiery Cross" at eleven o'clock at night.[214]

The *Asbury Park Press* noted that "elaborate precautions" were taken to ensure the event was "spy proof," with admittance granted only to members of the Klan and its affiliated organizations. "Everyone seeking admission will be requested to show their dues cards," the *Press* reported.

The elaborate celebration was yet another calculated theatrical effort by Arthur Bell "to impress upon thousands of visitors to the north Jersey shore resorts the strength of the hooded organization," according to a local news report. "The three-day celebration of the Klan is interpreted as an effort to widely advertise the Shark River reservation as a potential resort for Klansmen and members of affiliated organizations."[215]

Such events ensured the Klan remained a visible force in the area, at least for a brief time. Its presence, with all of the ominous implications, was heralded to local residents by a "huge electric cross made of steel and covered with light bulbs that emblazoned the night sky." Russ Henderson, who was born and raised in Wall Township, only a few minutes' walk from Klan headquarters, recalled that "every night you could see it for miles around."[216]

Bickering between Klan activists and Klan real estate entrepreneurs undermined the initial success of the highly publicized activity at the Marconi site. Klan activists claimed the Monmouth Pleasure Club was Klan property, while the deed holders, who happened to be local Klansmen, asserted the headquarters property was merely leased to the parent organization. The Klan reign proved to be a short one. By 1927, the dispute had become a bitter wrangle acted out in highly publicized court proceedings.

Arthur Bell was in the forefront of the fight for the Klan, working out of his living quarters in a comfortable bungalow on the tract. In October 1927, in a mimeographed letter to "all Klansmen, Klanswomen and Krusaders who are stockholders in the Monmouth Pleasure Club Association," Bell contended the Pleasure Club was formed by Klan members to secure a home for its members. "The stock was sold to our Klan and Krusader members," Bell wrote. "Lots have been sold because of the Klan events staged by the Klan, in fact, you have been told the Monmouth Pleasure Club Association was the Klan and you have supported it and paid large parts of your Klan revenue for that reason."[217]

Stockholders of the Pleasure Club, however, maintained that the property was purchased "as a business investment, pure and simple, and further that it was incorporated as such under the laws of New Jersey." In addition, "The understanding according to club members, was that the Klan was to pay a certain monthly rental for the privilege of holding

This "cottage" overlooking the Shark River inlet in Wall Township, once an office for the Marconi Company, was part of the Monmouth Pleasure Club property. One of the buildings was occupied by Arthur and Leah Bell before they were evicted following the successful Pleasure Club lawsuit against the national Ku Klux Klan. Today it is part of the InfoAge Museum. *From Joseph Bilby.*

meetings on the grounds and for the use of a bungalow for Grand Dragon Bell and his wife and for other Klan officials," the *Asbury Park Press* noted.[218]

To complicate matters, the national Klan joined the state organization's legal battle, supporting Bell's proposed resolution to require Pleasure Club directors to concede that the property belonged to the Klan. Pleasure Club members feared such a declaration would give the Klan "absolute control" over the property and that the land would ultimately end up in the hands of the national group. Bell, however, told his New Jersey constituents he was confident the national Klan would waive its rights to the property. Bell's detractors were skeptical, contending that the Grand Dragon was conniving to "throw the property into the hands of the national Klan organization and thereby enrich heads of the order on a magnificent scale." Considering the Klan's record in fiscal matters, and that Bell was a conniver of the first order, this was not an unwarranted assumption and was quite justified.[219]

A series of dizzying events in the fall of 1927 revealed that local Klan enthusiasm was on the wane and the organization's membership was on the brink of a precipitous decline. "The Klan ranks are thinning rapidly," noted the *Asbury Park Press* on October 5. "Asbury Park Klan No. 7 met last night on the Pleasure Club property and a number of resignations were received," the *Press* stated, adding that up to 50 members dropped out of the group. In addition, there were "whisperings of 50 or more resignations of women belonging to the auxiliary of the KKK." Although those resignations were ready to be handed in at the group's meeting, no action was taken because Leah Bell, who was head of the Kamelia, was out of town.[220]

The property dispute resulted in many Pleasure Club members dropping their membership in the Hooded Order. These departures, "by the score," saw themselves as strictly investors in the property at stake, with limited ideological links to the Ku Klux Klan. One such émigré was Harry H. Looker, a leading member of the Avon Taxpayers Association, who expressed his strongly held views over a different issue as he "created somewhat of a sensation last summer when he declared he would stand with a shotgun at the gates of the Ocean Grove Camp meeting resort to stop any automobilist who sought to run his car there on the Sabbath."[221]

The national Klan formally revoked the charter of the Point Pleasant chapter, claiming that all rights and property of the local Klavern had automatically reverted to the Atlanta headquarters due to the revocation. Amid the confusion, noted swindler and occasionally disbarred attorney Paul Wendell of Trenton, who claimed he represented the Point Pleasant chapter, an assertion disputed by the Pleasure Club, was legally removed from the case by the court.[222]

As Klan membership dropped, members of the Pleasure Club vowed to "tear apart" the Klan's contention of ownership "item by item." In response, a delegation of Klan members appeared at the meeting of the club's board of directors on October 20 to air their own grievances. In a document read at the meeting, the Klan representatives asserted that to be an original member of the Monmouth Pleasure Club, it was necessary to be a Klan member. The disgruntled Klan members went on to state that "because of the fact that the officers of the Pleasure Club had resigned from the Klan, they were no longer entitled to hold stock in the association property." The Klan delegates demanded that the property held by its "disbarred" members be returned to the Klan.[223]

Trenton attorney Paul Wendell was involved in numerous scams of the era, including the Lindbergh kidnapping case. He claimed to represent the Point Pleasant chapter of the Klan but was removed from the case by the court. *From Joseph Bilby.*

After the document was read, Grand Dragon Bell delivered a five-minute rant "in which he assailed the policy of the association." Following Bell's diatribe, Francis L. Stone, the Pleasure Club's board president, sought to tamp down the angry tone of the meeting when he "advised the protestants that the case had been duly taken down by a stenographer and that its content would be examined carefully by the board of directors. No answer was given to the demands or claims of the Klan at the meeting."[224]

Bell continued to make local headlines, particularly after an unfortunate reporter asked him to discuss the Klan's position on the land dispute. The Grand Dragon responded that he had no comment on the case and casually added that he was carrying a gun and asked whether the reporter was afraid. The intrepid interviewer responded that he was not frightened and was more interested in learning about recent developments in the property battle. Bell refused to provide any details. When shown a copy of a newspaper report on the board of directors' meeting, Bell said, "It's a good fiction story. I like good fiction stories."

The Grand Dragon eventually relented and offered a prepared statement, but only after he was assured it would appear exactly as he wrote it. The brief statement said, "That as the grand dragon of the Knights of the KKK, I transact my Klan business upon the floor of the klavern and not through the columns of the newspaper."[225]

The Klan's legal case was dealt a major blow in February 1928, when a federal judge dismissed a complaint filed by the national Ku Klux Klan that sought an injunction restraining the Pleasure Club "from taking any action with respect to the property which might prejudice the interests of the Klan."[226]

Several days after this defeat, a New Jersey Chancery Court decision rejected the Klan's claim to the property, bringing an end to "involved litigation in which the Klan accused the Pleasure Club of being only a holding corporation for it and then breaking faith." The court decision marked a "decisive victory for the club in its bitter fight for possession of the valuable development," a local newspaper noted.[227]

All that remained was the national Klan's appeal, which was dismissed by the United States circuit court of appeals in September 1929. The court declared that the Klan's contention of ownership of the Monmouth Pleasure Club was not based on any actual evidence and tellingly declared:

The property rights of the stockholders guaranteed to them under their charter and the laws of the state cannot be taken from them because of loose talk of irresponsible persons, and because, as the court said, "somebody somewhere said something to somebody" at some time. The facts before the court clearly showed that the declaration, whatever it was, of a trust was not in writing and is contrary to the Statute of Frauds in New Jersey.[228]

The career of Grand Dragon Bell paralleled the failing fortunes of the Klan, despite his continuing reputation for a "fiery tongue and boastful speeches," mostly directed at Al Smith as the property battle raged on. An April 1928, after this aggressive huckster fought so vigorously for possession of the Pleasure Club property, he suffered an ultimate, unsurprising indignity—eviction from his "comfortable cottage" on the estate. Furthermore, Klan members were forbidden to meet on the property, which required a relocation of their headquarters. They wound up in a threadbare office above an auto garage in Belmar.[229]

Bell's days of popularity and political influence seemed over, although he made a major effort to regain relevance during the presidential campaign of 1928. It was probably not a shocking news development when he resigned from his leadership position in January 1929. Imperial Wizard Evans denied any discord with Bell, noting, "He quit of his own volition." The *Asbury Park Press* was perhaps more insightful, noting that Bell's "power began to wane about two years ago" when the legal battle with the Pleasure Club began. The case indeed initiated the once seemingly unlikely unraveling of Bell's Klan career.[230]

As for the Pleasure Club as a real estate venture, individual sales plummeted during the Depression as the market collapsed. Newspaper advertisements announced bargain prices for housing lots on the property, designated as the "Imperial Park" subdivision of Wall Township, located between the Shark River Inlet and Hurley Pond Road. Bankruptcy ensued, however, and the remaining lots were sold at a sheriff's sale for failure to pay taxes in 1935. The former Marconi headquarters, with its hotel and bungalows, was eventually sold to the Young People's Association for the Propagation of the Gospel, a group that established a short-lived Christian Bible college on the site. During World War II, it became known as Camp Evans, a military research center substation of Fort Monmouth. This is how it remained until being turned over to local and county government use on the closure of Fort Monmouth in 2011.[231]

Today, while most of the old Pleasure Club land is occupied by suburban housing, the former headquarters property is known as the InfoAge Science History Learning Center and Museum. The location was redeemed by

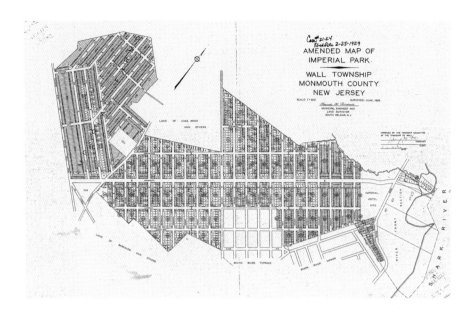

Above: Imperial Park property map in 1929. *From Monmouth County Clerk.*

Left: Times got tough for the Monmouth Pleasure Club as the Depression deepened. Although owned by current and former Klansmen, the organization was essentially a real estate business and cut prices in a vain attempt to keep the business going. *From Joseph Bilby.*

focusing on the facility's enormous importance during its incarnation as Camp Evans, when it played a key role in the development of radar as a weapon in World War II and when it opened space communications in 1946. The museum's mission is to "preserve, educate and honor scientific innovation and history to inspire new generations of thinkers, dreamers and visionaries." It is a State of New Jersey Historic Site and a National Historic Landmark.[232]

Indeed, it is ironic that a former haven of blatant bigotry and misinformation is now a museum dedicated to the efforts of a diverse group of men and women who contributed to the country's pursuit of education and scientific achievement. Long gone are the days when men and women

In a final bit of irony, the old Marconi Hotel, which became New Jersey Klan headquarters, is now the InfoAge Science History Learning Center and Museum. *From Joseph Bilby.*

of the "Hooded Order" gathered at this imposing edifice to promote their agenda of prejudice and exclusivity. Only the streets in Imperial Park that the Pleasure Club named in honor of American presidents—up to William Howard Taft—remain.

CHAPTER 8

"WE DON'T WANT ANY MORE OF THEM."

By the late 1920s, an egregious series of national and state scandals had weakened the Ku Klux Klan in New Jersey as well as nationwide. Many believed the bitter legal battle between the national organization and the Monmouth Pleasure Club over the Wall Township property would be the death knell for the New Jersey Klan.

After Grand Dragon Bell resigned in January 1929, a newspaper reported, "The national committee of the organization 'negotiated the resignation,' it is understood." The reason for Bell's action was not explained, and Imperial Wizard Evans insisted, against abundant public evidence, that "there has been no dissension in state Klan ranks" and "there is nothing wrong there." Evans assigned Hugh Kelly, Grand Dragon of the Realm of Vermont and New Hampshire, to come to New Jersey and "take charge of affairs until the election of a successor to Bell." Asked if that election would occur soon, the Imperial Wizard answered that he would wait "until the stew simmers down."[233]

It was evident that the Monmouth Pleasure Club debacle had resulted in the effectual "disintegration" of the New Jersey Klan, with expectations that the organization would "soon become a thing of the past." It also became clear that this caused Arthur Bell's exit, despite Evans's lack of acknowledgement. The Bells ended up in a West Belmar apartment following the abrupt eviction from their comfortable abode at the Pleasure Club. They eventually returned to Bloomfield, where Arthur reportedly opened a lunchroom, although he may also have served as "eastern representative for a household products company" while trying to maintain relevance with his anti–Al Smith tour. With Bell's resignation, the New Jersey Klan lost not only the services of its most effective public representative but also a tireless organizer in his wife, Leah.[234]

The weakened Jersey Klan, trying to maintain relevance after the loss of the Bells and its headquarters, stepped up a notch in its faux law enforcement role. When New Jersey state police raided an illegal liquor still in Buena in March 1929, they were surprised when six men, identifying themselves as Klansmen, "appeared out of the woods" and claimed they had been spying on the still and offered to help with the raid. The police did not need or want the assistance and declined, but the story made the local newspapers.[235]

That same month, the New Jersey Klan announced that its yearly convention and rally would be held on April 19 at the American Amity Club, a Klan property in Scotch Plains. In contrast to the hyper-inflated numbers of up to fifty thousand attendees predicted in the past, leaders estimated that five thousand Klansmen and women would attend the event. That number included "delegations" from "New York, especially Staten Island and Long Island, Connecticut, Delaware and Pennsylvania." There was no follow-up story on the gathering, suggesting attendance was minimal.[236]

Membership continued to decline. In July, Russell Tetley, newly elected Exalted Cyclops of the Red Bank Klan chapter, circulated a letter to lapsed Klan members with an appeal to remain in the order. After assuring the reader that he was not selling stock in the organization, Tetley pitched membership as a natural for "red-blooded Protestant Americans." He pointed out that "the Klan dues are but fifty-cents a month," and in return, members would be part of "an organization which stands as a Guardian of American principles and ideals" and would be able to share them through "the Fellowship of Klans-men, men of your own faith and race."[237]

There may have been more to the Bell resignation than met the public eye. In 1930, thirty-five-year-old Leah Bell moved back to her parents' home in Grand Rapids, Michigan, and shortly thereafter filed for divorce on grounds of "cruelty." Arthur did not contest the divorce, which was granted on August 28, 1930. It was kept from the public until November, when Bell married twenty-two-year-old Florence Kierstead, a secretary who had worked for him for several years. When asked for a comment, Leah Bell responded that the divorce was a "private affair." No doubt.[238]

Arthur Bell had returned to rabble-rousing by the time of his marriage to Florence. He had a new partner, William J. Simmons, founder of the second Klan, who had also been eased out of his position years before. Simmons

By 1929, membership in the Red Bank Klan had declined significantly. A few years before, as shown in this photograph, the chapter was riding high and even had its own band. *From Randall Gabrielan.*

later created and incorporated the Caucasian Crusaders of the White Band, subsequently shortened to the White Band, which was described as a "new organization to keep the white race supreme." The White Band dropped the anti–Catholic and Jewish tropes of the Klan and opened membership to all white males over the age of eighteen. The group fed upon the increasing anxiety of Americans, caused in no small part by the beginning of the Great Depression. In such an atmosphere, it was easy to exploit race and point to African Americans and Asians as the cause of job loss by white men.[239]

Although "Generalissimo" Simmons claimed the White Band was founded several years earlier, the group did not make the national news until the summer of 1930, when a spat arose between Simmons and some of his partners. Despite internal dissension, Simmons recruited around the country for his new group. Arthur Bell became the organization's "Superintending Ambassador" for New Jersey.[240]

In addition to touting race supremacy, the White Band targeted political radicals who arose from the ruins of a collapsed economy. One White Band leader riled up his audience by saying, "Shall America be and remain white and American, or shall it mongrelize, communize, degenerate and die?" He condemned what he called "America's mischief-making Siamese quadruplets—black radicalism, red communism, yellow intrigue and white asinine folly."[241]

The press, inured to Klan antics for a decade, was unimpressed with White Band bloviating. One paper headlined Simmons's new effort as "Klucker Tries a New Racket" while dismissing his claim that he had 350,000 members. Early on, the White Band encountered official disapproval in the Northeast when "national department of mobilization chief of staff" Arthur Jesup was arrested in New York City for "soliciting funds without a license" in an attempt to collect money he claimed would assist the unemployed in the deepening Depression. When questioned by officers of the city's Department of Public Welfare, Jesup admitted he had no idea what the money would actually be used for and was told to leave town on the next train."[242]

Arthur Bell hosted his first White Band rally at Wemrock Park, near Freehold, New Jersey, on November 7, 1930, and invited a reporter to attend. Before a crowd of 250 people, he denied that he bore any ill will toward the organization he formerly led, saying, "I still believe in its principles. If, since I left it, it became a tattered remnant, the blame is not on my shoulders." Bell's statement was analogous to the "and Brutus is an honorable man" disclaimer, though. He accused his Klan successor, Grand Dragon William I. Morgan, of undermining him, without providing specifics. Bell's theme was echoed by special guest William J. Simmons, who also derided Morgan and called on New Jersey Klansmen to "come back to your daddy," Arthur Bell, and join the White Band.[243]

Simmons then launched into a racist rant, "alluding in a general way to black, red and yellow menaces and to sinister and powerful organizations plotting the undoing of the white race, both within and without the country." His virulence claimed that all of America's woes were due to race, complaining:

A rising tide of color is rushing up to swamp the white man. One of every eight is now colored. Huge companies exist for the sole purpose of smuggling in Japs and Chinamen. They are being landed by the thousands, and the companies get $150 to $200 a head. There is also a flood of Mexicans and low-grade greasers flowing into the country. We educate them, give them the benefits of our civilization, and every time they take a job, a white man goes down.[244]

In fact, Chinese immigration to the United States had been banned since the Chinese Exclusion Act of 1882, while restrictions were expanded to ban virtually all Asians in an immigration law in 1924. That legislation, strongly supported by the Klan, also severely restricted immigration from Southern and Eastern Europe, so Simmons's rant was, unsurprisingly, fearmongering at its worst or a lie at its best. Once you instill fear in people, however, they are more easily manipulated.

Arthur Bell returned to his old Jersey shore bailiwick in 1931 with a vigorous campaign intended to create a viable White Band organization in the state. At Long Branch in August, he supported the city commissioners in their decision to ban Communists from conducting "street corner meetings." In September, two hundred people attended his picnic in Lakewood to celebrate his wedding anniversary to his second wife. Bell, never

William Joseph Simmons, seen here as head of the White Band, appeared at Monmouth County's Wemrock Park with Arthur Bell, the organization's New Jersey "Superintending Ambassador," in November 1930. *From Joseph Bilby*.

one to miss an auspicious occasion, announced at the event that he had been elevated to the rank of "provost marshal general" of the national White Band. He also took the opportunity to announce his plans for holding a series of "anti-Communist meetings in Lakewood and Asbury Park in the near future."[245]

On October 8, Bell held a meeting for White Band members at the Improved Order of Red Men's Hall in Point Pleasant. There, speakers declared that America's "social, political and financial structure" was "threatened by Communism, corruption, crime and other factors which are 'de-Americanizing.'" Bell charged Monmouth and Ocean County officials with graft and corruption, echoing Simmons and claiming without evidence that "there is a boat that brings aliens to this shore every two weeks. We notified the immigration department, but nothing was done."

Alton Milford Young, Bell's crony from his Klan days who had moved from Belmar to Jersey City and was now White Band "director of propaganda of the national department of mobilization," also spoke. Young claimed that "right in Asbury Park young, innocent girls are being kept against their will in houses of ill-fame." He proposed a solution to the problem by suggesting that every American over the age of twenty-one be photographed and fingerprinted.[246]

Meanwhile, the State of New Jersey initiated a program likely to strike fear at the core of the Klan and White Band and in the hearts of their members. In 1930, no African Americans served in the New Jersey National Guard, and the segregated United States Army had no plans to authorize a black Guard battalion or regiment in the state, though there were a few such units in other states. Prominent New Jersey African Americans—notably William D. Nabors from Orange—petitioned their state legislators to create a state-funded organization, and Assemblyman Frank S. Hargraves responded with the introduction of a bill. On April 16, 1930, both houses of the New Jersey legislature passed Chapter 149, Laws of 1930, authorizing the "organization and equipment of a battalion of Negro infantry" at the state's expense. Committees were established on July 14, 1931, to organize the first companies of what came to be called the First Separate Battalion, New Jersey State Militia. Companies were assembled in Newark, Atlantic City and Camden. The battalion later added a band based in Atlantic City and a medical detachment in Newark.[247]

The First Separate Battalion gained a sterling reputation. The unit was training at the Sea Girt National Guard Camp on September 8, 1934, when the cruise ship *Morro Castle* caught fire and anchored in turbulent seas two miles off Sea Girt. Panic-stricken passengers and crew made desperate attempts to launch lifeboats while others jumped overboard in efforts to save themselves from the flames. Governor A. Harry Moore, who was ending the season at his official summer residence in the National Guard camp, ordered the black militiamen to the beach as part of local rescue efforts. Braving hurricane-like conditions, they rescued survivors and recovered bodies drifting to shore. Officers who were morticians in civilian life established an improvised morgue in the camp that soon held seventy-eight bodies.[248]

The black Jerseymen were cited by Governor Moore and the state legislature for their "courage, courtesy, and sympathetic handling of a very gruesome duty," and the city commissioners of Atlantic City presented Company B with a bronze plaque "in recognition of its heroic and devoted services to the community, state and nation."[249]

The battalion also distinguished itself in other venues, winning numerous athletic and marksmanship trophies. In 1936, the adjutant general persuaded the New Jersey state senate to re-designate the battalion as an adjunct unit of the New Jersey National Guard, and in May 1937, the First Separate Battalion, New Jersey State Militia was renamed the First Battalion, New Jersey Guard. As World War II approached, the battalion was formally accepted by the federal government as a National Guard unit and

Members of the African American First Separate Battalion on the rifle range at the New Jersey National Guard Camp in Sea Girt. *From National Guard Militia Museum of New Jersey.*

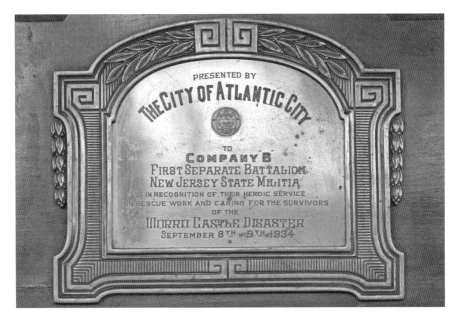

The plaque presented to the members of the Atlantic City Company of the First Separate Battalion who aided in the rescue of survivors of the *Morro Castle* disaster. *From National Guard Militia Museum of New Jersey.*

renumbered as the First Battalion of the National Guard's 372nd Infantry Regiment, composed of African American guardsmen from Washington, D.C, Maryland, Massachusetts and Ohio. The unit was mobilized and served in World War II.[250]

The First Separate Battalion refuted everything William J. Simmons, Arthur Bell, the White Band and the Ku Klux Klan claimed, which explains their reason for ignoring its existence. While the black Jerseymen of the First Battalion were proving their "Americanism" beyond a doubt, the White Band began its descent into the same sewer as the New Jersey Ku Klux Klan. Membership in either organization—minimal at best—was impossible to determine at the time and remains so. The White Band sputtered on until the middle of the decade, attracting little notice other than a newspaper report in March 1933 that declared "a class of 41 candidates" would be initiated into the order at a meeting at Red Men's Hall in Point Pleasant.[251]

The Klan also experienced a deep decline in news coverage in New Jersey during the early 1930s. Despite efforts to remain relevant and recruit, as one report put it, the "death blow was coming." Nationally, Klan membership was estimated at a mere forty-five thousand, down from a claimed several million

Officers and noncommissioned officers of the First Separate Battalion's Company C at Sea Girt in 1935. *From National Guard Militia Museum of New Jersey.*

in the previous decade, reflecting a massive crash over the course of a few years. In Newark, where the Klan had once boasted two thousand members, and still claimed a—likely inflated—membership of three hundred, local headquarters at a frame house at 410 Bergen Street was foreclosed on in May 1931 for failure to pay the mortgage.

In Union County, where "Klan activities had faded," local Klan property in Scotch Plains, including "a large clubhouse, bowling alleys, dance hall and three acres of land," was subjected to a sheriff's foreclosure sale in April 1932, as taxes and assessments had gone unpaid on the property for three years. The only highlight was in July 1932, with the creation of a new chapter in Morristown, the Jockey Hollow Klan No. 23, with sixty-two members.[252]

In November 1931, Grand Dragon Morgan wrote to erstwhile New Jersey Klansmen imploring them to return to active membership. He advised that he would be holding gatherings around the state and looked forward to "meeting personally" with inactive members and former members and talking to them "quietly and secretly." Morgan attempted to inspire with flattery, claiming that only men who possessed "fine fiber" and could "measure up" to Klan standards were receiving his correspondence. He implored their need to respond, return to the Klan and engage in the "furtherance of the protection of our government."[253]

Morgan, apparently taking a cue from the White Band, stressed the Klan's opposition to Communism to a conservative audience apprehensive about the rise of militant and radical labor in the wake of the Depression. He invited national Klan lecturer W.A. Hamlet to a meeting in Middletown in October 1932, where Hamlet endorsed President Herbert Hoover's reelection and warned his audience that there was collusion between Communists and Democrats to elect Franklin D. Roosevelt. Other meetings around the state endorsed Hoover, despite the evident lost cause of his candidacy. In one optimistic turn, members of the Somerset County Klan were able to regain their Owanamassee Country Club property, which had been sold to the Liberty Packing Company in 1931 and turned into a rabbit farm. Although the club hosted occasional Klan events, for the next decade the owners leased it out for income-producing activities, including weddings and parties unconnected with the Klan, as well as a Boy Scout camporee.[254]

The year 1933 opened inauspiciously for the Vineland Klan, with the arrest of Klansman Louis A. Maudlin for impersonating a police officer. Maudlin was directing traffic at a Klan meeting dressed in a police uniform with a "whistle suspended from his neck and a cavalry officer's badge adorning his chest." When he saw approaching police, Maudlin tried to hide behind his car, but to the amusement of local journalists, they nabbed him.[255]

Imperial Wizard Evans tried to revive the national Klan in 1934 with the announcement of an anti-Communist offensive, which created some confusion in New Jersey. Arthur Bell, who foresaw personal gain in implied association with the Klan's new crusade, conducted a Communist condemnation tour of Monmouth and Ocean Counties with his buddy Reverend Young. At an open-air meeting in Point Pleasant's Brisbane Field, he was introduced as "the superintendent of one hundred anti-Communistic groups in New Jersey." The White Band was never mentioned by name. The Bell tour had been alluded to in the press as part of the Klan's national outreach, but Grand Dragon Morgan issued a statement clarifying that neither Bell nor Young were Klan members.[256]

In southern New Jersey, the Klan revived its vigilante promises with a pledge to aid Charles F. Seabrook in "eliminating Communistic agitators among striking farmworkers at Bridgeton." Most Seabrook workers were African Americans or Italian immigrants, so intimidating them aligned with Klan doctrine. However, Seabrook's hired thugs and the local police, armed with clubs and tear gas, were able to do the job without Klan assistance.[257]

The only significant media mention the New Jersey Klan obtained in 1935 was Grand Dragon Morgan's announcement of an Easter Sunrise Service to be held at the Owanamassee Country Club. Morgan began 1936, however, with a bombastic pledge to "rid the country of undesirable aliens." He claimed that "there are three million five hundred thousand foreigners in the United States illegally and that a means should be found for their deportation." Morgan asserted that deporting those people would result in more jobs for native-born Americans. Naturally, he did not explain how he would accomplish that task. Several months later, he blamed the Lindbergh kidnapping on the lack of a "proper investigation" of convicted kidnapper Bruno Hauptmann. Morgan averred that Hauptmann had not been properly vetted when he immigrated to the United States.[258]

The Klan's highlight in 1936 was, once again, the Easter Sunrise Service at the recovered Owanamassee Country Club. Klan leaders, exaggerating as usual, told the newspapers they expected ten thousand attendees. Hiram Evans was booked to lecture on "Orderly and Constitutional Government." Grand Dragon Morgan was expecting to host Grand Dragons from eight northeastern states. The numbers failed to meet expectations, as only around three thousand people "from many parts of the east" appeared at the service, and only "about half of them" were in Klan regalia.[259]

Right: Reverend Alton Milford Young was a Baptist minister who became Arthur Bell's right-hand man. He left the Klan, joined the White Band and then returned to the Klan along with his boss. *From Joseph Bilby*.

Below: In June 1934, Seabrook Farms in Cumberland County, New Jersey, used a force of hired thugs or "deputies" supplemented by local police to attack African American and Italian immigrant strikers, as seen here. Area Klansmen offered their assistance in crushing the strike but were not needed. *From Joseph Bilby*.

In 1937, Klan corporate headquarters in Atlanta claimed that the organization was "growing by leaps," boosted by advocacy for "buy American, the eradication of communism, deportation of aliens holding American jobs until every American is employed, better public schools and white supremacy." Although silent, the tattered New Jersey branch presumably agreed. Despite the upbeat message, the national Klan had also encountered severe fiscal difficulties and sold off most of its property. The "Imperial Palace" in Atlanta was purchased by an insurance company, which in turn sold it to the Catholic Church. The Christ the King co-cathedral for the Savannah-Atlanta diocese was built on the site in 1939. In what the *Atlanta Constitution* called "a new spirit of tolerance," Imperial Wizard Evans attended the dedication ceremony by invitation. Evans arrived in a suit rather than a robe and was photographed shaking hands with Cardinal Dennis Dougherty, archbishop of Philadelphia, who dedicated the new church.[260]

In October 1937, Klan founder "Colonel" Simmons provided a far different analysis of the organization's standing than Klan headquarters.

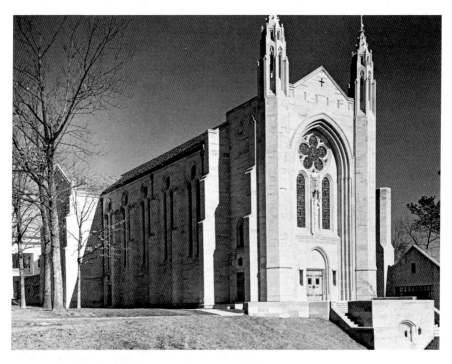

The co-cathedral of Christ the King, built on the site of the former Ku Klux Klan national headquarters in Atlanta. *From Joseph Bilby.*

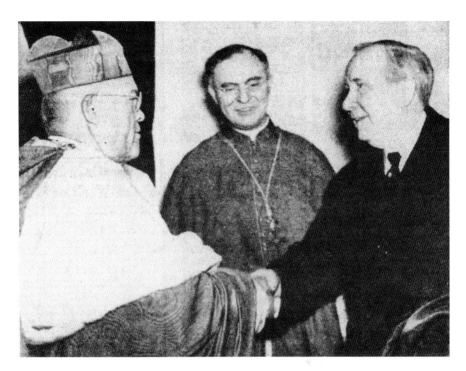

Above: In what the newspapers called "a new spirit of tolerance," Imperial Wizard Hiram Evans (*right*) shakes hands with Cardinal Dennis Dougherty at the dedication of the Atlanta Catholic co-cathedral on former Klan property in 1939. *From Joseph Bilby*.

Right: Frank Cheeseman, acquitted of murdering his girlfriend's mother, had a cross burned on his lawn by unknown persons in 1939. The *Asbury Park Press* published in an editorial, "We don't want any more of them." *From Joseph Bilby*.

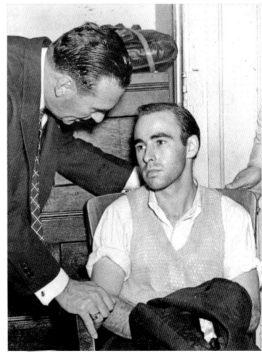

Simmons, while recovering from an illness at a veterans' hospital in Atlanta, told a reporter that "the Klan today is all bluff." He claimed that he had lost his leadership post in 1922 due to "traitors," presumably led by Hiram Evans. Simmons also expressed his hope to lead the Klan "back to its original aims."[261]

As the decade ended, the New Jersey Ku Klux Klan was viewed as a vestige of the past preferably forgotten, even in its former Monmouth County bastion. However, another incident would force a recollection. Neptune resident Frank Cheeseman, acquitted of murdering his girlfriend's mother in October 1938, served a six-month sentence for carrying a concealed weapon without a permit. After his release, Cheeseman returned to Neptune, where some local citizens set a cross afire on his lawn and fled the scene. The incident led the editorial staff of the *Asbury Park Press*, recalling Klan activity in the previous decade, to opine, "During the heyday of the Ku Klux Klan we became familiar with the burning cross and learned to abhor it as a peculiarly cowardly means of terrifying citizens. We don't want any more of them."[262]

CHAPTER 9

"IT WAS ONE OF MY AWFUL BLUNDERS."

An editorial printed on April 14, 1939, in both the *Freehold Transcript* and the *Monmouth Inquirer* derided the Ku Klux Klan's attempts to rekindle public interest and support. "This is a mistake not only because money in poor men's pockets is too scarce to be wasted on dues, robes, etc., but because we all want a square deal," the writer noted. "Any organization which panders to bigotry, intolerance and such evils and endeavors to usurp the perogatives [*sic*] of our courts of law and equity is as un-American as the most blatant 'ism' organization." This view exemplified the increasing hostility and impatience of the press toward thinly veiled bigotry; the scales were falling off the eyes of the population at large as well.[263]

The Klan's ongoing membership exodus was not limited to ordinary members abandoning the organization. Hiram Evans resigned his position as Imperial Wizard after attending the dedication of the Catholic cathedral on former Klan property in Atlanta. Shortly afterward, he said off the record, "I was not a fool. I wanted out. This was a good exit." James A. Colescott succeeded Evans as Imperial Wizard on June 10, 1939. Colescott, who was depicted by one reporter as "flushed and porky," had served his Klan internship under Indiana Grand Dragon Stephenson and became the first Imperial Wizard to work his way up through the ranks.[264]

By the late 1930s, the steady decline of the New Jersey Klan was turning into its death throes, as was the case with the national organization, although the group's diminishing number of loyalists continued to promote its agenda. The Klan's efforts were increasingly met with anger, disgust and ridicule.

After Arthur Bell disappeared along with the White Band following his 1934 speaking tour, media mention of him all but vanished. The occasional single-line notices in the *Asbury Park Press* noted that a friend from the shore was visiting him in Bloomfield.

Since Hiram Evans had presided over Bell's departure as leader of the New Jersey Klan, Colescott's elevation probably permitted Bell's reappearance as a Klansman in October 1939. Then Bell, who billed himself as King Kleagle of the New Jersey Realm, declared the group's intention to hold a mass meeting at Journal Square in Jersey City later that month. In response to Bell's proposal, a *Jersey Journal* editorial vehemently declared that it had been "emphatically demonstrated"

James A. Colescott, who succeeded Hiram Evan as the Ku Klux Klan's Imperial Wizard, probably enabled the return of Arthur Bell. *From Joseph Bilby.*

that Journal Square was not an appropriate venue for such a gathering. "Disruption that would be caused to business and traffic can in no way be justified," the newspaper noted.[265]

The editorial concluded with a scathing condemnation of the organization, stating, "The Klan is getting off on the wrong foot in its move to organize in Hudson County—probably because the KKK has no right foot to get off on. Everything about the KKK, from bedsheets with peepholes to tar and feathers and intolerance, is wrong stuff for real Americans." Public outcry, coupled with official hostility, stymied the Klan's plan, and probably fortunately for the Klansmen in heavily Catholic and immigrant Jersey City, the rally was never held. In December 1939, however, Bell conducted a "Lodge of Sorrow" service commemorating deceased Klan members in Jersey City—the home of his faithful associate Reverend Alton Milford Young.[266]

The Klan, despite increasingly stiff opposition, persisted in maintaining a somewhat visible presence in New Jersey. When thirty Klan members, led by Arthur Bell clad in a golden robe, gathered together on February 12, 1940, in Wanaque, they were greeted by the "boos of milling townsfolk" and were pelted with eggs as they left the meeting. When Klan leaders held a meeting at the Roselle Park municipal building later that year, ten policemen stood

Arthur Bell, once again leading the New Jersey Ku Klux Klan, conducted a "Lodge of Sorrow" memorial service for deceased members of the organization in Jersey City in December 1939. *From Joseph Bilby.*

guard throughout the building to prevent any acts of violence against the group of about twenty-five members.[267]

On May 30, 1940, in Mountainview, Bell, who had apparently promoted himself to "Grand Giant of the Ku Klux Klan," claimed that he and the Klan were on the lookout for a "Fifth Column" movement in the United States. The term "Fifth Column" originated during the Spanish Civil War, when a Nationalist general advancing on Madrid told a reporter that he had four columns attacking the city and one within it. "Fifth Column" was used to refer to any group seeking to undermine a nation or government from within.[268]

A staggering Klan even resorted to its old tactic of using fiery crosses to intimidate its racial, religious and political targets. On the night of June 29, 1939, Klansmen torched a large wooden cross near the railroad tracks by South Avenue in Westfield. Three men in Klan regalia distributed pamphlets that outlined the rationale for the cross burning "to keep America out of war, to protect our Constitution, to retain our race integrity, to preserve Protestant patriotism, to fight Communist activities, to make German-Americans, Italian-Americans, etc., just good Americans." The robed men were arrested but later released. Meanwhile, two similarly attired men set up a kerosene-soaked cross in another part of town, then set it ablaze. The perpetrators disappeared before police could apprehend them. That same night, a third cross was set on fire in Elizabeth.[269]

Such acts of intimidation inspired others not formally affiliated with the Klan but certainly of a kindred mindset. One of the most disturbing offenses occurred in August 1939, when a group of white men, "imitating Ku Klux Klan methods," tried to drive seven African American farm workers out of Cranbury. Two of the victims, Mr. and Mrs. Francis Preston from Coleman, Georgia, were smeared with white paint and were later taken to a hospital to remove the paint without injury to their skin. The other five workers "were stripped of their clothing near the shack where they lived" and, after being told to "get back down south where you belong," were taken to a nearby highway and ordered to "start walking." There, someone fired a shotgun, frightening the workers, who fled to a nearby field and hid.[270]

The attack set off a state police investigation, and "indignant farmers joined the police in a search for the perpetrators." The probe led to the arrest of nine men who pleaded guilty to stripping and painting the farm workers. The men were given two- to three-year suspended sentences by Judge Adrian Lyon, "who told the defendants their actions were mob lynch [sic] psychology and a disgrace to the country."[271]

Such local incidents of bigotry were potentially nerve-wracking for an American public besieged by increasing reports of brutality abroad, as Nazi Germany fulfilled its agenda of persecuting Jews and other "undesirables." Inevitably, Klan members embraced the prejudice and intolerance of Nazism. As early as 1933, popular entertainer Will Rogers had remarked on the similarities between the two hate-filled movements. "Papers all state Hitler is trying to copy Mussolini," he wrote. "Looks to me like it's the Ku Klux that he is copying. He doesn't want to be emperor; he wants to be Kleagle."[272]

Throughout the 1930s, Klansmen frequently praised Hitler. At a Klan rally in Westchester County, New York, an unidentified, masked speaker said, "Hitler has appreciated the evil influences of the Jews and has realized that most of them are Communists." In Miami, a local Klan member noted, "When Hitler has killed all the Jews in Europe, he's going to help us drive all the Jews on Miami Beach into the sea!"[273]

The Klan's admiration of Nazi Germany intensified throughout the 1930s and culminated in a joint rally that proved disastrous for the New Jersey branch and its leader, Arthur Bell. The rally was held in conjunction with the German-American Bund, an American version of the Nazi Party whose members dressed in Nazi-style uniforms and gave each other the fascist salute. The leader of the Bund during the height of its power in the late 1930s was Fritz Kuhn, a swaggering Munich-born chemist and World War I German army veteran who demanded absolute obedience from his followers. Like Kuhn, most Bund members were recent, post–World War I immigrants, not members of America's older, largely assimilated German-American community.[274]

Kuhn's initial negotiations with the New Jersey Klan to stage the rally were cut short in 1939 when he was arrested for embezzling more than $14,000 from the Bund treasury, part of which went to support his mistress. Negotiations continued, however, with newly appointed Bundesfuhrer G. William Kunze and his deputy August Klapprott. The joint event was

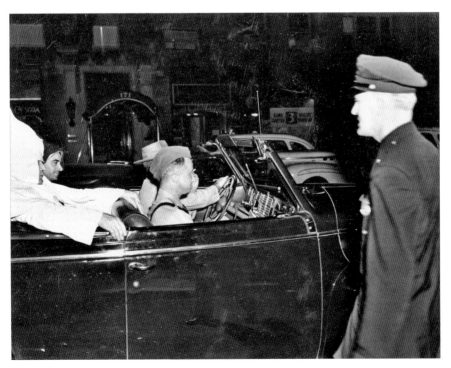

Klansmen and Bund members drove into New York City in September 1941 to attend an "America First" rally at Carnegie Hall but were "warned away" by police officers. *From Joseph Bilby.*

agreed upon by Klapprott, Bell and E.J. Smythe, who was the director of the Protestant War Veterans Association and a close ally of both the Bund and the Klan.[275]

The rally was scheduled to be held at the Bund's two-hundred-acre Camp Nordland near Andover, New Jersey. The camp was a bizarre fantasy world of Nazism, dominated by a large, yellow frame recreation hall, adorned inside with a prominent picture of Hitler. Camp gatherings were characterized by blatantly outrageous behavior, as illustrated by an appearance by Kuhn on September 4, 1938. Holding the rapt attention of a crowd of two thousand Bund members and their guests, Kuhn called for a "socially just, white, gentile-ruled United States" that prohibited Jews from holding "positions of importance" in government. He also demanded a "thorough cleansing" of the Hollywood film industry and the "outlawing of the Communist party in the United States."[276]

Perhaps the greatest success of Kuhn's rabble-rousing was raising the ire of many Americans. He also sparked consternation in some German Nazi officials who had come to realize that the Bund was a political liability. The Germans were eager to maintain the goodwill of Americans as they continued to build a military force in violation of treaties and to make war-like moves in Europe. Thus, German leaders issued a formal statement to disavow the Bund. Zealous American Bund members simply ignored the German protests.[277]

In New Jersey, energetic opposition to the Bund grew in the late 1930s, spearheaded by organizations that included the Non-Sectarian Anti-Nazi League of Newark, the German-American League for Culture, the Jewish-American War Veterans, the American Legion and the "Minute Men," a group of hardened boxers and gangsters organized by well-known crime figure Abner "Longie" Zwillman in Newark's Third Ward. Zwillman, who had made a fortune as a bootlegger during prohibition and controlled most of the rackets in the city, unleashed his tough *schtarkers* on Bund meetings to crack Nazi heads. Many German-American descendants of nineteenth-century immigrants increasingly regarded the Bund as an embarrassment, while officials and residents who lived near the Nordland camp displayed their animosity in multiple ways, from revoking the camp's liquor license to hurling rocks at Bund members.[278]

Public toleration in New Jersey had become shaky by the time the Bund and Klan held their joint rally on August 18, 1940. Nearly two hundred Klansmen and several hundred of their friends and relations were met at the camp by some eight hundred Bundsmen, and they were "graciously escorted

The "Minute Men," a group of hardened boxers and gangsters organized by well-known organized crime figure Abner "Longie" Zwillman in Newark's Third Ward, marching in front of Schwaben Halle on Springfield Avenue in Newark. Bund members were meeting inside on October 27, 1938. *From Joseph Bilby.*

around the grounds by storm troopers dressed in black trousers, white shirts and black ties." Klapprott and Bell met on a platform "and smilingly shook hands." As storm troopers equipped with brass knuckles stood guard over the crowd, Klapprott extended a welcome to the "anti-war, pro-Americans who had the courage to attend the rally." Klan members expressed sympathy for members of the Bund "who had been 'persecuted' for their adherence to the doctrines of Nazi Germany."[279]

Toward the end of the rally, a crowd of about five hundred Sussex County residents "gathered at the camp gate and intermittently attempted to drown out proceedings by singing the Star-Spangled Banner." The fury intensified in the following days, when national Klan officials expressed their dismay over the joint rally and ousted Bell and Young from the organization. Ordering the immediate removal of both men, Imperial Wizard Colescott asserted that Bell permitted "a high officer of the German-American Bund" to address the gathering and that both Bell and Young "failed to live up to the ideals of the Klan in their management" of the meeting. "There can be no sympathy" between the Bund and the Klan, he added. Bell, "brimming with indignation," responded that Colescott had known about and approved of the rally.[280]

Colescott's censure was only the beginning of new difficulties for the New Jersey Klan. Newspaper editors expressed their anger, and the *New York Times* demanded that both the Klan and Bund be put under "close and constant surveillance." A concerned Congress turned the matter over to the House Un-American Activities Committee, commonly referred to as the Dies Committee after the chairman, Representative Martin Dies Jr. of Texas. The committee had been created as an investigative panel on Communism and Fascism. [281]

The committee began its investigation of the Bund-Klan merger attempt in October 1940, with a hearing in Newark. Klapprott denied any formal ties between the Klan and Bund. Bell agreed, and when asked what he thought about a Klan-Nazi merger, Bell responded that he had "thought it a good idea at the time, but I don't now." Bell's expulsion from his leadership position and the intervention by the Dies Committee squelched further cooperation between the New Jersey Klan and the Bund.[282]

The ensuing years were tumultuous for both groups. In 1941, New Jersey attorney general David Wilentz authorized the Sussex County sheriff to raid the Nordland property, shutting it down as a public meeting place. This was authorized by a New Jersey statute that empowered authorities to close "every building or place where the law is habitually violated." During the raid, sheriff's officers and twelve deputized members of the local American

Arthur Bell (*left*) and August Klapprott on the stage at the Bund/ Klan rally at Camp Nordland, in Sussex County, New Jersey, on August 18, 1940. *From Joseph Bilby.*

Legion Post confiscated a quantity of Bund emblems, letters, maps and photographs of Hitler and ordered about one hundred picnickers and weekend residents of the camp's bungalow colony to pack up and leave.[283]

Bundesfuhrer Kunze and several other key members of the organization were arrested and indicted by a Sussex County grand jury for violating a 1935 law prohibiting the promotion of hatred based on race or religion. Although the New Jersey Supreme Court overturned the charges, the Bund's days were numbered. After the United States instituted a military draft in September 1940, Bund members were accused of counseling men on how to avoid service, prompting many to scatter, including Kunze, who fled to Mexico. Following the American entry into World War II, the now deflated Fritz Kuhn was sent to an internment camp in Texas. In 1946, he was released and deported to West Germany, where he died in 1951.[284]

The Klan also endured mounting scrutiny and public hostility following the 1940 rally debacle, particularly since its message of divisiveness threatened the pressing demand for national unity during the war years.

After a secret Klonvocation was held on April 23, 1944, Imperial Wizard Colescott announced that the Klan had disbanded as a national organization. "This does not mean the Klan is dead," Colescott claimed. "We simply have released local chapters from all obligations, financial and otherwise, to the imperial headquarters. I am still imperial wizard. The other officials still retain their titles, although, of course, the functions of all of us are suspended. We have authority to reincarnate at any time."[285]

Good riddance, an *Asbury Park Press* editorial proclaimed. "The decline of the Klan was inevitable because it preached a doctrine of intolerance," the editorial stated. "Some may call the Klan a casualty of war, but to fair-minded citizens this is just another way of saying that when the chips were down America found that whites and blacks, Protestants, Catholics and Jews could fight side by side, and they didn't need a Klan to spur them on."[286]

For the first time since 1915, America would be rid of an organized national Ku Klux Klan. But the respite would be brief. Following the defeat of the Axis powers, the Klan once again insinuated itself into the national political scene. "Fiery Cross of KKK Burns Again in South," trumpeted a headline in the *Asbury Park Press* on October 21, 1945. "The Ku Klux Klan, claiming a membership of more than 20,000 in Georgia, is burning its fiery cross again and stirring up new arguments over the order born in Reconstruction days," the article stated. Klan members lit a "huge cross," visible for sixty miles, atop historic Stone Mountain. It was the first cross burning since the outbreak of World War II.[287]

Grand Dragon Dr. Samuel Green, Colescott's successor, said the Georgia Klan had halted cross burning during the conflict because it was necessary "that all factions unite to win the war." Green took offense from an editorial in the *Macon News*, which said the renewed Klan activity brought "a feeling of hopelessness, of futility, of fighting against an unseen enemy of law and order." Green countered that the Klan was a law-abiding organization that was valiantly fighting Communism. He added that police raids in Atlanta had uncovered Communist pamphlets "promising the whole South" to black citizens if they joined the party.[288]

After the war, rumors of a Klan resurgence in New Jersey were squelched when Governor Walter Edge finally got revenge for the Klan's opposition to his Senate candidacy in the 1920s. Edge requested that his attorney general, Walter D. Van Riper, propose that the Klan should be outlawed as "an organization destructive of the rights and liberties of the people" and that its 1923 incorporation papers in the state be revoked. Van Riper brought the matter before the New Jersey Supreme Court, testifying that the Klan "does advocate the arousing of social and religious prejudices, fomenting disorder and encouraging riots and unlawful assemblies in contempt of the state of New Jersey." Justice A. Dayton Oliphant wrote a decision granting the attorney general's request on October 9, 1946. Van Riper described his action to journalists as a "preventative" measure based on newspaper statements made by a Klan official in Georgia who said the Klan might be revived in New Jersey.[289]

By now, the man of many titles, Arthur Bell, doubted the feasibility of a Klan resurgence, telling an inquiring journalist that "the Klan is dead beyond recognition." He envisioned a place for "an organization along Klan lines, but it must be carefully organized, embracing this time the Catholic and Jew, as well as the Protestant." African Americans, he suggested, "should be placed in an auxiliary."[290]

A.M. Young, Bell's former colleague, took greater steps to distance himself from the Hooded Order. In 1948, the former Baptist minister was confirmed

New Jersey attorney general David Van Riper (*left*) informing Georgia assistant attorney general Daniel Duke of how he quashed revival of the Ku Klux Klan by initiating a "show cause" petition in August 1946. This enabled New Jersey Supreme Court justice A. Dayton Oliphant to issue a "certificate of ouster," ending the Klan's corporate legal existence in the state. *From Joseph Bilby.*

as a member of the Roman Catholic Church in a ceremony at St. Aedan's Parish in Jersey City. As he leaned on a cane, the white-haired, sixty-one-year-old Young told a reporter that his association with the Klan "was one of my awful blunders." He said that he became a Catholic because he found "sympathy and understanding" in the Church.[291]

Despite signs that times were changing, however, the Klan's bitter legacy of bigotry and bullying lingered. In 1948, a twelve-foot cross was set ablaze in front of the home of Leroy Hutson, a black radio engineer who lived only a few miles from the former Klan headquarters in Wall Township. Hutson was an employee of Camp Evans, the high-level army research facility on the former Monmouth Pleasure Club property. Described by police as a "decent man," Hutson, who lived in Wall Township with his wife and infant son, discovered the blazing cross outside his living room window. Despite his acknowledgement that "it was a terrifying experience," Hutson insisted that he had no intention of moving. State police placed a guard at his residence and made the rounds of surrounding homes, warning neighbors to keep off his property.[292]

The *Central Jersey Home News* reflected the public's disgust with the incident, noting that although there was no evidence the Klan was involved in the cross burning, "the intent of those erecting the fiery cross was the old despicable KKK intent to bring fear to the heart of the Negro who has taken up residence in a predominantly white neighborhood."[293]

In the decades that followed, such displays became a rarity, particularly as African Americans campaigned for their rights as citizens. Indeed, by 1965, an *Asbury Park Press* writer observed that "news stories about the Ku Klux Klan seem as far removed…as the war in Kashmir or the political doings in Indonesia." The *Press* added that many residents of the New Jersey Shore assumed an organization like the Klan "can't happen here." Older residents "with long memories—and deep local roots—are aware, though, that it not only could—but did—happen here." Many of those old-timers no doubt remembered the Klan's heyday when Arthur Bell indulged grandiose fantasies from his luxurious headquarters in Wall. The era of public troublemaking and cross burnings was brief, but it left a dark imprint on New Jersey history. "While it flourished…the Klan was a force to be reckoned with," the *Asbury Park Press* noted. "Still and all, the historical fact remains: It did happen here."[294]

CONCLUSION

Who in New Jersey would have been interested in joining the 1920s iteration of the Ku Klux Klan? And why? As with most historical questions, the answer is complicated. Founded in 1915, the new Klan intersected a period in history in which many trends in popular culture and politics were merging, bringing results both beneficial and damaging. It was indeed a "Lost Generation" era in more ways than are usually imagined, and many people seeking assurance would find themselves in unfortunate associations.

The pioneering, and coincidentally proselytizing, film *The Birth of a Nation* characterized Klansmen as heroes and solidified and expanded the post-Reconstruction "Lost Cause" theme beyond its southern birthplace. At the core of the lost causers' view of history were the ideas that the Civil War was caused by a debatable constitutional issue and that Reconstruction involved northern scoundrels who manipulated dimwitted former slaves into persecuting southern whites. This self-serving mythology was pervasive enough to be accepted by academic historians of the era, including southern-born President Woodrow Wilson. Some continue to accept this false and hollow interpretation today.

Racism, a heritage created out of the necessity to justify race-based slavery by casting enslaved people as inherently inferior, was endemic to the white American mindset of the time. It was handed down like family china without question, although it did vary dramatically in intensity and practice between the Deep South and northern states like New Jersey. Northern racist views could be subtle or oblique. For example, the Federal Writers' Project 1939 Works Progress Administration (WPA) guidebook to the state referred to the residents of the mixed-race community of Gouldtown as "hard working, highly respected people" but noted that they "refuse to accept a Negro status but cannot be classified as whites." Unfortunately, the general acceptance of eugenics by many in the academic community added another layer of discrimination and led to the fear of racial and ethnic "mongrelization."[295]

Such insidious beliefs found fertile soil in the early twentieth century, a time when "other-directedness," a phenomenon Harvard sociologist David Riesman identified in *The Lonely Crowd*, was on the ascent. Due to alienation caused by the war, industrialization, shifting social roles and economic statuses, people were desperate to fit in, reinforce their own values and find validation in groups that reflected a mythic better day in the past. New Jersey was as impacted as anywhere in America.

Patriotic and fraternal organizations, such as the Klan, were popular in the late nineteenth and early twentieth centuries. They provided bonds of brotherhood and a sense of self-importance to members who may have needed stimulation in otherwise mundane lives. They provided entertainment and fellowship, as well as affordable, if minimal, life insurance and occasional aid to family members in need. In the late nineteenth century, although vaudeville theaters and "opera houses" were being built across the nation, public amusement in many rural areas was limited to traveling carnivals, and there was no government safety net for working and middle-class folks. These organizations filled a void—to some degree—and paved the way for the rise of the Klan in the society that evolved after World War I. Fraternal organizations were also racially and religiously restricted. For example, the Improved Order of Red Men would only admit white men, and African Americans formed their own societies in response. So, the racial and religious exclusionary limitations of Klan membership were not viewed as unusual.

In the nineteenth century, the United States also saw a recurring fear of immigrants, particularly Catholics. The ethnicity of arrested persons was published in newspapers, and immigrants, particularly poor Irish ones, were thus associated with crime. Catholics were also feared as being agents of the pope, determined to make the United States a theocracy. Only Protestants could legally hold public office in New Jersey until 1844.

Such prejudices led to anti-immigrant riots in various areas, including New Jersey. In the 1850s, a gang known as the "Short Boys" attacked a German immigrant picnic in Hoboken with guns and clubs, and a Catholic church in Newark was burned down shortly afterward. The creation and growth of the American or Know Nothing Party in the pre–Civil War years reflected this unease, and New Jersey elected former Whig and American Party member William A. Newell governor in 1856. The Junior Order of United American Mechanics (JOUAM), founded in 1853, was a large anti-Catholic and anti-immigrant fraternal organization that provided insurance as well as an orphanage for members' families. The order's stances on immigrants and Catholics mirrored those of the 1920s iteration of the Klan, and since multiple memberships in fraternal organizations was not unusual, many JOUAM members also became Klansmen.

Anti-immigrant fever waxed and waned, typically in correlation with economic conditions and immigration trends. In the forty years prior to the Klan's appearance in New Jersey, immigration from Eastern and Southern Europe dramatically increased. Many newcomers, primarily Catholics and Jews, did not speak English, while some were radical socialists and anarchists. This raised the anxiety level among native-born, white Protestants.

As if ordinary fear of immigrants was not enough, in the 1920s, Henry Ford, a highly regarded industrialist whose success did not negate his lack of awareness of history or his nativist beliefs, printed a half million copies of a translation of the tsarist secret police's anti-Semitic forged document, *The Protocols of the Elders of Zion*. This was purportedly the guidebook of an international Jewish conspiracy to conquer the world by gaining control of the media and business while subverting the morals of gentiles. Ford also published a series of anti-Semitic articles in his newspaper, the *Dearborn Independent*. In 1927, Ford was forced by ensuing economic and legal challenges to disavow his assertions, but there is no evidence he was personally contrite.

Latent public fear was exacerbated by World War I and its aftermath. George Creel, President Wilson's appointee as head of the United States Committee on Public Information, launched a massive propaganda offensive to convince Americans, many of whom questioned their country's participation in the conflict, that the enemy was the embodiment of evil. Creel's organization, with little regard for the truth, created a feeling of paranoia and "us versus them" not only directed at enemies abroad but also at perceived ones at home. Immigrants from Germany and Austria-Hungary were particularly suspect. Opponents, real or imagined, were at times treated harshly, often without regard to due process.

The Bureau of Investigation, the forerunner of the FBI, used vigilante volunteers to track down draft-dodging "slackers" and anyone who questioned American involvement in the war. Postwar events, including the Wall Street bombing and the "Red Scare," during which Attorney General Palmer arrested and deported accused radicals, most of them recent immigrants, created a mindset where vigilantism and spying on internal "enemies," along with a disregard for the details of law, merged with anti-immigrant hysteria.

The feared postwar breakdown of old-fashioned morality, coupled with other aspects of the Roaring Twenties like bootleggers, speakeasies and jazz, with its roots in African American music, added to the xenophobia created by Creel and Palmer and created a deep sense of cultural apprehension among traditionalists.

The rise of the Klan could be perceived as a rejection of change and modernism. Thus, the Klan could represent nostalgia for the "good old days," when minorities and women knew their places in society and the King James Version Bible was the basis of all true religion. In July 1927, Dr. William Hiram Foulkes, a Newark Presbyterian minister who was not known to be a Klansman, encapsulated this apprehension when he condemned "trial marriage, unchaste courtship and easy divorces," as well as jazz, which he decried in a thinly veiled racist rant as "jungle music, fetid with jungle odors, sensuous with jungle motions and inflamed with jungle passions."[296]

Jazz gave Klansmen an opportunity to hit at another of their perceived enemies—the New York City songwriters who produced "Jew-monopolized jazz" as part of a concerted effort to lower moral standards through inflamed "animal passions." Broadway musical theater also, according to Klan publications, produced "songs that rock with sex" and "filthy suggestion" of vulgarities that undermined pure Protestant womanhood. However, the Klan did have a taste for music, as their gatherings regularly featured Klan Bands. The bands played more than religious music, as the organization endorsed some dancing and popular songs, including the foxtrot "Ain't We Got Fun" and the nonsense song "Yes, We Have No Bananas." They even used the latter tune's melody as a cover with Klan lyrics. They also composed their own songs, including one by New Jersey Klansman Kenneth Patterson, who wrote "KKK—If Your Heart's True It Calls to You."[297]

New Jersey Klan members had many reasons for joining the organization, and entertainment was certainly one. Surely some members, including the owners of the Monmouth Pleasure Club and the Owanamassee Country Club, viewed the Klan as an entrepreneurial business vehicle. People like Arthur Bell likely saw an opportunity to make money and a chance to feed their megalomania through grandiose behavior, attempting to gain national recognition. Bit players included minor-league shysters like the Rawson brothers of Bergen County, who used the opportunity to

Right: Dr. William Hiram Foulkes exploited cultural apprehension and espoused thinly veiled racism when he condemned "trial marriage, unchaste courtship and easy divorces," as well as jazz, which he decried as "jungle music, fetid with jungle odors, sensuous with jungle motions and inflamed with jungle passions." *From Joseph Bilby*.

Below: German-American Bund leaders after their arrest at Camp Nordland in 1941. *Left to right*: Mathias Kohler, Wilhelm Kunze, August Klapprott and Bund attorney W.V. Keegan. *From Joseph Bilby*.

The sheet music for "KKK—If Your Heart's True, It Calls to You" by Kenneth A. Patterson, published in Avon by the Sea, New Jersey. *From Joseph Bilby.*

participate in theatrics and promote their own local importance; politicians like Basil Bruno, who saw votes to mine; and community pastors who may have believed the Klan was a vehicle to return the wayward from speakeasies to pews. Others were struck by fear of social change wrought by immigrants or local economic concerns, while still others surrendered to peer pressure.

Some early Klan success was probably inspired by patriotic zeal. In addition, Klan religious beliefs were not all that different from those of the average middle-class, small-town American. Thus, patriotism and religion enabled some to overlook the Klan's over-the-top rhetoric, especially in a state like New Jersey where the Klan repeatedly protested that it was a civic organization, albeit one dressed in unusual attire, determined to "clean up" aspects of a wayward society. The average New Jersey initiate was probably attracted to what appeared to be an entertaining, patriotic secret society with a selective membership replete with arcane rituals, hocus pocus and ostentatious costuming. Such trappings would make him feel significant and provide an opportunity to network for economic improvement. He was not, despite modern views clouded by memories of the Klan of the 1950s and 1960s, looking to join a violent lynch mob. His casual bigotry was not only

Klan affiliation could be a business booster or breaker, depending on the market and region. This cigar advertisement was a direct product pitch to Klansmen. *From Joseph Bilby*.

accepted by most mainstream white Americans of his day but was endemic throughout American social culture.

For the most part, the New Jersey Klan recruit was not prone to violence, as was certainly the case in other states, limiting himself to melodramatic and intimidating acts of cross burning. In fact, there was far more violence committed against the New Jersey Klan than by it. In the 1990s, historian Randall Gabrielan interviewed an elderly New Jersey woman who was the "widow of a suspected Klansman." Without disclosing any family connection, she opined that "she did not understand why the Klan was looked upon so harshly now as they did not seem so bad at the time." Gabrielan responded that "It depended on who you asked." One historian of the New Jersey Catholic community noted that while there was "little outright violence" from the Klan, "ugly rhetoric, threats and fear-mongering stained community life in religiously and racially mixed places" around the state.

Despite the incompetence of the New Jersey Klan, along with claims of piety and patriotism, New Jersey Klansmen do not merit exoneration. In the final analysis, they allied themselves with a national organization that was based on hate, fueled by fear and practiced intimidation. Numerous New Jerseyans of the era were vocal in their opposition.[298]

How many members were in the New Jersey Ku Klux Klan? Kenneth T. Jackson in his 1967 book, *The Ku Klux Klan in the City, 1915 to 1930*, projected sixty thousand at its peak, a number that has been accepted by most historians. Jackson admits, however, that his numbers are "personal estimations" based on newspaper reports and Klan sources of questionable reliability. The Klan, on both national and state levels, regularly exaggerated and lied on many issues, especially membership numbers. Jackson also notes that his totals, in addition to being guesses, cover "all male and female persons initiated into the Klan between 1915 and 1944."

The actual number of New Jersey Klan members at any given time is unknowable due to a lack of surviving records, but it was certainly far less than Jackson posited. Contemporary accounts reveal that the numbers of Klansmen claimed as attending a particular New Jersey rally or parade were invariably exaggerated, even with a considerable infusion of out-of-state attendance.[299]

Linda Gordon remarked in *The Second Coming of the KKK* that "a study of the Indiana Klan showed that few, other than leaders, stayed for long. In one town, out of 1,067 listed as Klavern members, 61.5 percent had been suspended at least once for non-payment of dues." If this was the case in the state featuring the most powerful Klan membership, then it follows that New Jersey's rates were comparable, or perhaps greater. For many, the novelty probably wore off rather quickly.[300]

Why did the Klan collapse in New Jersey? The state, with its large immigrant population, many of whom were Catholics and Jews, was not a hospitable venue. The opportunistic local politicians who joined or affiliated themselves with the Klan only did so in the limited areas of Klan strength and quickly abandoned the organization after its fall. Unlike in other states, New Jersey officeholders of both parties at the state and national levels not only distanced themselves from the Klan but in many cases publicly condemned it.

Violent opposition in Bound Brook, Perth Amboy and elsewhere no doubt gave many people second thoughts as well. While the national and state organizations became mired in scandals, their ensuing public relations disasters, including the cases of D.C. Stephenson, George Lawson and Roscoe Ziegler and the climactic legal battle for the Monmouth Pleasure Club property, compounded problems for the New Jersey organization. In addition, the violence perpetrated by Klansmen in other states may have given former supporters second thoughts. Despite the anti-crime and anti-corruption bloviating, it was also clear that the Klan had not "cleaned up" anything. And then came the Great Depression, which changed the focus of the nation.

In the following years, many New Jerseyans wanted to erase the story of the Ku Klux Klan from the state's historical memory. For example, the WPA Guidebook mentions the organization only once, comparing it—without being state-specific—to the "dour and bitter" anti-immigrant groups of the nineteenth century.[301]

The final straw broke when Arthur Bell, a veritable New Jersey *Zelig* who, like the fictional Woody Allen character, showed up everywhere, popped up again in 1940, trying to merge the ragged remnants of his organization with the German-American Bund. Fears about a revival in the postwar era resulted in a formal legal end to the Klan in the state when Attorney General Van Riper had its New Jersey incorporation papers revoked. The Ku Klux Klan and New Jersey were never, nor could they ever be, to paraphrase a former state tourism slogan, "perfect together."

NOTES

Chapter 1

1. *Trenton Times*, November 10, 1915; *New Brunswick Home News*, February 26, 1916; *Courier News*, February 27, 1918.
2. MacLean, *Behind the Mask*, 4; Gordon, *Second Coming of the KKK*, 12.
3. Chalmers, *Hooded Americanism*, 28.
4. Gordon, *Second Coming of the KKK*, 12, 185.
5. Ibid., 13.
6. Ibid., 14, 15; Chalmers, *Hooded Americanism*, 32.
7. Oklahoma Commission, *Tulsa Race Riot*.
8. Chalmers, *Hooded Americanism*, 37–38.
9. *Issues of To-Day* (NGMMNJ Archives, September 1, 1921).
10. Harcourt, *Ku Klux Kulture*, 15–18.
11. MacLean, *Behind the Mask*, 5; Chalmers, *Hooded Americanism*, 32.
12. Chalmers, *Hooded Americanism*, 33–35.
13. *Trenton Times*, August 25, 1920.
14. *Asbury Park Press*, March 5, 1920; Bridgewater *Courier News*, September 17, 1921.
15. *Trenton Times*, August 1, 1921.
16. Ibid.; *Trenton Times*, August 11, 1921; *New Brunswick Home News*, August 20, 1921; Bridgewater *Courier-News*, September 21, 1921.
17. Bridgewater *Courier-News*, September 17, 1921.
18. Lurie and Mappen, *Encyclopedia of New Jersey*, 404.
19. Irwin, *State and Its Government*, 3–4.

20. *New York Times*, August 30, 1921; Jackson, *Klan in the City*, 178.
21. *Asbury Park Press*, September 13, 1921.
22. *Newark Evening News*, August 30, 1921.
23. *Newark Evening News*, September 14, 1921.
24. Ibid.
25. Ibid.

Chapter 2

26. *New Brunswick Home News*, May 16, 1922; *Ocean Grove Times*, May 26, 1922.
27. *Asbury Park Press*, June 8, 1922.
28. Ibid.
29. Zimmer, *Immigrants Against the State*, 50–53; *New Brunswick Home News*, June 22,1922; *New York Times*, June 22, 1922.
30. Chalmers, *Hooded Americanism*, 242–44.
31. Murray, "Home in Hillsdale."
32. Gordon, *Second Coming of the KKK*, 14–16.
33. Ibid., 16–17.
34. *New York Times*, September 9, 1922.
35. *Chatham Press*, October 7, 1922.
36. Ibid.; *New Brunswick Home News*, October 2, 1922.
37. Kunstler, *Hall-Mills Murder*, 333. The Kunstler theory has been thoroughly debunked, most convincingly by Gerald Tomlinson in *Fatal Tryst*, 313–15.
38. Tomlinson, *Fatal Tryst*, 313–15.
39. Ibid.
40. Ibid.
41. *New York Times*, December 23, 1922.
42. *Asbury Park Press*, December 9, 1922.

Chapter 3

43. *Asbury Park Press*, February 16, 1923.
44. *Newark Evening News*, February 24, 1923.
45. *Newark Evening News*, February 24, 1924.
46. *Asbury Park Press*, April 10, 1923.
47. *Red Bank Register*, May 30, 1923.
48. *Time Magazine*, October 22, 1928; *Time Magazine*, July 8, 1946.
49. *Time Magazine*, July 8, 1946; *Red Bank Register*, April 6, 1921.
50. *Red Bank Register*, April 6, 1921; Harcourt, *Ku Klux Kulture*, 21.

51. *The Good Citizen* 14, no. 2 (February 1926).

52. Harcourt, *Ku Klux Kulture*, 65.

53. *New Brunswick Home News*, May 2, 1923.

54. Ibid.

55. Ibid.

56. Ibid.

57. Ibid.; Jamison, *Religion in New Jersey*, 143.

58. *New York Times*, May 3, 1923.

59. Ibid.

60. *Red Bank Register*, June 6, 1923; *Asbury Park Press*, May 21, 1923.

61. *Asbury Park Press*, May 21, 1923.

62. Ibid.

63. Ibid.

64. Ibid.

65. *Asbury Park Press*, May 11, 1923.

66. *Asbury Park Press*, May 25, 1923.

67. Ibid.

68. *New Brunswick Home News*, August 25, 1923.

69. *New York Times*, May 31, 1923; *Asbury Park Press*, July 5, 1923; *Red Bank Register*, July 18, 1923; *Red Bank Register*, July 25, 1923.

70. Pine, Hershenov and Lefkowitz, *Peddler to Suburbanite*, 183; Fred Byrnes interview with the author, November 12, 2014; Murray, "Home in Hillsdale."

71. *Bridgewater Courier News*, December 16, 1922.

72. Murray, "Home in Hillsdale."

73. Frederick (MD) *Daily News*, June 26, 1923.

74. *Asbury Park Press*, July 10, 1923; *Asbury Park Press*, July 30, 1923; *Red Bank Register*, June 13, 1923.

75. *New Brunswick Home News*, August 25, 1923.

76. *Asbury Park Press*, July 16, 1923.

77. *New Brunswick Home News*, August 25, 1923.

78. Ibid.

79. Ibid.

80. Furer, "Perth Amboy Riots."

81. Ibid.; *Asbury Park Press*, June 5, 1923; *New Brunswick Home News*, June 16, 1923.

82. *Asbury Park Press*, August 31, 1923; *Freehold Transcript*, September 7, 1923.

83. *Freehold Transcript*, September 7, 1923.

84. Furer, "Perth Amboy Riots"; *Asbury Park Press*, August 31, 1923; *New York Times*, August 31, 1923; *New York Times*, September 1, 1923.

85. Joseph M. Boa interview with author, February 20, 2018.

86. *Newark Ledger*, August 31, 1923.

87. *New York Times*, January 12, 1923.

88. *New York Times*, November 23, 1923; *Atlantic City Daily Press*, January 14, 1923.

89. Camden *Courier Post*, August 13, 1924.

90. Undated newspaper clipping, courtesy Frank Tomasello.

91. *New York Times*, July 24, 2018; *New Brunswick Home News*, September 9, 1923.

92. *Newark Evening News*, November 27, 1923; *Newark Evening News*, October 18, 1923.

93. *Ocean Grove Times*, October 19, 1923.

94. *Red Bank Register*, December 5, 1923.

95. *Asbury Park Press*, December 10, 1923.

96. Ibid.; Wade, *Fiery Cross*, 193–94.

97. *Asbury Park Press*, December 10, 1923; Chalmers, *Hooded Americanism*, 245.

Chapter 4

98. *New York Times*, January 15, 1924.

99. Linderoth, *Gangsters on Vacation*, 42–44.

100. Ibid., 50; Mappen and Saretzky. *Prohibition in New Jersey*, 26–27.

101. Jackson, *Klan in the City*, 179.

102. Wade, *Fiery Cross*, 224–25.

103. *Asbury Park Press*, July 24, 1923.

104. *New York Times*, April 7, 1924; *Asbury Park Press*, April 8, 1923.

105. *Asbury Park Press*, April 8, 1923.

106. *Asbury Park Press*, April 8, 1924; *Asbury Park Press*, April 18, 1924; *Asbury Park Press*, August 2, 1924; Wolff, *4th of July*, 184.

107. *Newark Evening News*, March 19, 1924.

108. *New York Times*, January 15, 1924.

109. Ibid.; November 16, 1925, Indenture transfer, Monmouth County Archives.

110. *Asbury Park Press*, July 2, 1924; *Ocean Grove Times*, July 4, 1924.

111. *Asbury Park Press*, July 5, 1924.

112. Ibid.

113. Ibid.

114. Ibid.; *Keyport Weekly*, July 11, 1924; Federal Writers' Project, *Entertaining a Nation*, 137.

115. *New Brunswick Home News*, July 5, 1924.

116. Federal Writers' Project, *Entertaining a Nation*, 136.

117. *New York Times*, August 5, 1924.

118. Bridgewater *Courier News*, July 16, 1924.

119. *Asbury Park Press*, July 28, 1924.

120. *New York Times*, September 2, 1924.

121. Fleming, *New Jersey: A History*, 165–66.

122. *Asbury Park Press*, October 27, 1924.

123. Bridgewater *Courier News*, November 2, 1924.

Chapter 5

124. Freehold *Transcript*, February 18, 1925.

125. Kuntz, "George H. Lawson," 42–50.

126. Ibid.

127. Ibid.

128. Ibid.

129. Ibid.

130. Ibid.

131. Ibid.

132. Bridgewater *Courier News*, March 16, 1925; Harcourt, *Ku Klux Kulture*, 149.

133. Gordon, *Second Coming of the KKK*, 17–18.

134. Ibid., 193.

135. Ibid., 194.

136. Ibid.

137. *Asbury Park Press*, July 31, 1925.

138. Ibid.

139. *Asbury Park Press*, July 30, 1925.

140. *Asbury Park Press*, July 31, 1925.

141. *Asbury Park Press*, October 8, 1925.

142. *Red Bank Register*, March 11, 1925; *Red Bank Register*, March 18, 1925; *Red Bank Register*, April 15, 1925.

143. *Newark Evening News*, March 9, 1925.

144. *Asbury Park Press*, May 11, 1925.

145. Ibid.; *Ocean Grove Times*, May 15, 1925.

146. *Ocean Grove Times*, May 15, 1925.

147. Chalmers, *Hooded Americanism*, 247.

148. *Asbury Park Press*, May 22, 1925.

149. *Asbury Park Press*, June 1, 1925.

150. Ibid.

151. Ibid.

152. Murray, "Home in Hillsdale."

153. Ibid.

154. *New Brunswick Home News,* July 14, 1925.

155. *Asbury Park Press,* July 20, 1925; *Ocean Grove Times,* July 24, 1925.

156. *Asbury Park Press,* July 18, 1925; Harcourt, *Ku Klux Kulture,* 123.

157. Murray, "Home in Hillsdale."

158. *Asbury Park Press,* September 21, 1925.

159. *Bernardsville News,* September 3, 1925; Bridgewater *Courier News,* September 8, 1925.

160. *Asbury Park Press,* October 20, 1925.

161. Ibid.

162. *Asbury Park Press,* November 6, 1925.

163. Ibid.; Bridgewater *Courier News,* March 10, 1926; Bridgewater *Courier News,* March 12, 1926.

164. *Red Bank Register,* October 21, 1925; Gabrielan, *Red Bank,* 104.

Chapter 6

165. *Asbury Park Press,* March 18, 1926.

166. Ibid.

167. Mappen, *Prohibition Gangsters,* 121.

168. Sanger, *Autobiography,* 366–67.

169. Bridgewater *Courier News,* March 24, 1926.

170. Ibid.

171. *Asbury Park Press,* June 16, 23, 1926.

172. *Asbury Park Press,* June 12, 1926.

173. *Asbury Park Press,* July 14, 1926.

174. *Asbury Park Press,* September 13, 1926; Chalmers, *Hooded Americanism,* 289.

175. *Asbury Park Press,* November 4, 1926.

176. Ibid.; *JOUAM Fellowship Forum 1926,* Bush Collection.

177. *JOUAM Fellowship Forum; Asbury Park Press,* October 28, 1926; *Asbury Park Press,* November 4, 1926; Chalmers, *Hooded Americanism,* 290.

178. Chalmers, *Hooded Americanism,* 248; Gordon, *Second Coming of the KKK,* 213, 215.

179. Bridgewater *Courier News,* January 21, 1927.

180. *Asbury Park Press,* July 18, 1927.

181. *Bernardsville News,* April 14, 1927; *Bernardsville News,* April 21, 1927.

182. *Bernardsville News,* April 21, 1927.

183. Ibid.

184. Ibid.

185. Ibid.

186. *Asbury Park Press*, February 23, 1928.

187. Ibid.; *Asbury Park Press*, February 28, 1928.

188. Bridgewater *Courier News*, April 23, 1928.

189. Ibid.

190. *Encyclopedia of Alabama*, s.v. "Robert Stell Heflin," by Kevin Spann, last modified December 6, 2016, http://www.encyclopediaofalabama.org/article/h-3758.

191. Ibid.

192. Minneapolis *Star*, March 6, 1928.

193. Bridgewater *Courier News*, July 23, 1928.

194. Ibid.

195. Ibid.

196. Spann, "Robert Stell Heflin."

197. *Asbury Park Press*, June 1, 1928.

198. *New Brunswick Home News*, June 10, 1938.

199. *Asbury Park Press*, August 28, 1928.

200. *Asbury Park Press*, September 8, 1928.

201. Coleman, "Religious Liberty."

202. Bridgewater *Courier News*, October 31, 1928.

203. Ibid.

204. *Newark Evening News*, October 30, 1928; *Newark Evening News*, November 6, 1928.

Chapter 7

205. *Asbury Park Press*, October 3, 1925.

206. Ibid.; *Asbury Park Press*, October 22, 1925.

207. *Asbury Park Press*, October 22, 1925; *Asbury Park Press*, March 14, 1925; Original Pamphlet, courtesy InfoAge Science History Learning Center and Museum

208. Ku Klux Klan promotional brochure, InfoAge Science History Learning Center and Museum; land sales contract, Monmouth County Clerk's office.

209. *Asbury Park Press*, May 23, 1925

210. Ku Klux Klan promotional brochure, InfoAge Science History Learning Center and Museum.

211. Ku Klux Klan questionnaire, InfoAge Science History Learning Center and Museum.

212. *Asbury Park Press*, March 14, 1925.

213. Ibid.; *Asbury Park Press*, June 20, 1926.

214. Ku Klux Klan program, InfoAge Science History Learning Center and Museum.

215. *Asbury Park Press*, June 20, 1926.

216. Russ Henderson, oral history interview, InfoAge Science History Learning Center and Museum.

217. *Asbury Park Press*, October 4, 1927.

218. Ibid.

219. Ibid.; *Asbury Park Press*, October 5, 1927; *Asbury Park Press*, October 9, 1927.

220. *Asbury Park Press*, October 9, 1927; *Asbury Park Press*, October 5, 1927; *Asbury Park Press*, October 7, 1927.

221. *Asbury Park Press*, October 9, 1927.

222. *Red Bank Register*, February 3, 1928.

223. *Red Bank Register*, October 7, 1927.

224. *Asbury Park Press*, October 21, 1927.

225. Ibid.; *Asbury Park Press*, October 22, 1927.

226. Bridgewater *Courier News*, February 28, 1928.

227. *Asbury Park Press*, February 17, 1928.

228. Knights of the Ku Klux Klan v. Monmouth Pleasure Club Ass'n Inc, et al. (3rd Cir. September 19, 1929).

229. Ibid.; *Asbury Park Press*, October 9, 1927.

230. Knights v. Monmouth Pleasure Club; *Asbury Park Press*, January 22, 1929.

231. Knights v. Monmouth Pleasure Club; *Asbury Park Press*, April 5, 1935.

232. www.infoage.org.

Chapter 8

233. *Asbury Park Press*, January 29, 1929.

234. Ibid.

235. Bridgewater *Courier News*, March 21, 1930.

236. Ibid.; Bridgewater *Courier News*, March 31, 1930.

237. July 3, 1929, Moss Collection, Monmouth University Library.

238. Michigan Department of Health Bureau of Records and Statistics, *Divorce Record, Docket 33166*, August 28, 1930.

239. *The Oshkosh* (WI), August 27, 1930.

240. *San Bernardino County* (CA) *Sun*, July 28, 1930.

241. Marshall (TX) *News Messenger*, August 8, 1931.

242. Decatur (IL) *Herald*, August 5, 1932.

243. *Asbury Park Press*, November 8, 1930.

244. Ibid.

245. *Asbury Park Press*, August 21, 1931; *Asbury Park Press*, September 15, 1931.

246. *Asbury Park Press*, October 8, 1931.

247. Luzky, "History, 1ˢᵗ Battalion."

248. Ibid.

249. *New York Times*, September 10, 1934.

250. Luzky, "History, 1ˢᵗ Battalion."

251. *Asbury Park Press*, March 22, 1933.

252. *Newark Evening News*, May 27, 1931; *Bernardsville News*, April 7, 1932, *Bernardsville News*; July 28, 1932.

253. November 9, 1931, Moss Collection, Monmouth University Library.

254. Bridgewater *Courier News*, October 5, 1932; *Asbury Park Press*, October 25, 1932; *New Brunswick Home News*, June 9, 1941.

255. Vineland *Daily Journal*, February 15, 1933.

256. *Asbury Park Press*, September 13, 1934.

257. Bridgewater *Courier News*, July 7, 1934.

258. *Asbury Park Press*, January 9, 1936; *New Brunswick Home News*, April 10, 1936.

259. *New Brunswick Home News*, April 3, 1936; *New Brunswick Home News*, 13, 1936.

260. *New Brunswick Home News*, September 20, 1937; Wade, *Fiery Cross*, 264–65; *Atlanta Journal Constitution*, January 19, 1939.

261. Bridgewater *Courier News*, October 31, 1937.

262. *Asbury Park Press*, December 7, 1939.

Chapter 9

263. *Freehold Transcript*, April 14, 1939; *Monmouth Inquirer*, April 14, 1939.

264. Wade, *Fiery Cross*, 265.

265. Bridgewater *Courier-News*, October 20, 1939.

266. Ibid.

267. Ibid.; Bridgewater *Courier-News*, February 13, 1940.

268. Louisville *Courier Journal*, May 31, 1940.

269. Bridgewater *Courier News*, June 30, 1939.

270. *New Brunswick Home News*, August 13, 1939.

271. Bridgewater *Courier News*, September 30, 1939.

272. Wade, *Fiery Cross*, 266.

273. Ibid., 268.

274. Bilby, Madden and Ziegler, *Hidden History*, 125.

275. Wade, *Fiery Cross*, 270.

276. Bilby, Madden and Ziegler, *Hidden History*, 126, 129.

277. Ibid., 129.
278. Ibid., 129, 130.
279. Wade, *Fiery Cross*, 271; *Central New Jersey Home News*, August 19, 1940.
280. *New Brunswick Home News*, August 19, 1940; Wade, *Fiery Cross*, 271, 272.
281. Wade, *Fiery Cross*, 271, 272.
282. Ibid., 272.
283. Bilby, Madden and Ziegler, *Hidden History*, 30.
284. Ibid., 130.
285. Bridgewater *Courier-News*, June 5, 1944.
286. *Asbury Park Press*, June 7, 1944.
287. *Asbury Park Press*, October 21, 1945.
288. Ibid.
289. *Asbury Park Press*, October 10, 1946; *Freehold Transcript*, August 2, 1946; *Monmouth Inquirer*, August 2, 1946.
290. *Philadelphia Inquirer*, October 11, 1946.
291. *Asbury Park Press*, October 18, 1948.
292. Bilby, Madden and Ziegler, *Hidden History*, 117.
293. *New Brunswick Home News*, June 17, 1948.
294. *Asbury Park Press*, October 24, 1965.

Conclusion

295. Federal Writers' Project, *Guide to Its Present*, 637.
296. *The Bend* (OR) *Bulletin*, July 7, 1927.
297. Harcourt, *Ku Klux Kulture*, 124–25, 132.
298. Randall Gabrielan, email message with author, June 20, 2018; Regan, *Gothic Pride*, 173.
299. Jackson, *Klan in the City*, 237.
300. Gordon, *Second Coming of the KKK*, 67.
301. Federal Writers' Project, *Guide to Its Present*, 120.

BIBLIOGRAPHY

Books

Bilby, Joseph G. *Sea Girt: A Brief History*. Charleston, SC: The History Press, 2008.

Bilby, Joseph G., and Harry Ziegler. *Asbury Park: A Brief History*. Charleston, SC: The History Press, 2009.

Bilby, Joseph G., James M. Madden and Harry Ziegler. *Hidden History of New Jersey*. Charleston, SC: The History Press, 2011.

Chalmers, David M. *Hooded Americanism, the History of the Ku Klux Klan*. 3rd ed. Durham, NC: Duke University Press, 1987.

Federal Writers' Project, comp. *Entertaining a Nation: The Career of Long Branch*. Bayonne, NJ: Jersey Printing Company, 1940.

———. *New Jersey: A Guide to Its Present and Past*. New York: Viking Press, 1939.

Fleming, Thomas. *New Jersey: A History*. New York: W.W. Norton and Company, 1977.

Gabrielan, Randall. *Images of America: Red Bank*. Vol. 2. Charleston, SC: Arcadia Press, 1996.

Gordon, Linda. *The Second Coming of the KKK: The Ku Klux Klan of the 1920s and the American Political Tradition*. New York: Liveright, 2017.

Harcourt, Felix. *Ku Klux Kulture: America and the Klan in the 1920s*. Chicago: University of Chicago Press, 2017.

Irwin, Leonard B. *New Jersey: The State and Its Government*. New York: Oxford Book Company 1942.

Jackson, Kenneth J. *The Ku Klux Klan in the City*. New York: Oxford University Press, 1965.

Jamison, Wallace N. *Religion in New Jersey: A Brief History*. New York: D. Van Nostrand, 1964.

Kunstler, William M. *The Hall-Mills Murder Case*. New Brunswick, NJ: Rutgers University Press, 1980.

Linderoth, Matthew R. *Prohibition on the North Jersey Shore: Gangsters on Vacation*. Charleston, SC: The History Press, 2010.

Lurie, Maxine, and Marc Mappen, eds. *Encyclopedia of New Jersey*. New Brunswick, NJ: Rutgers University Press, 2004.

MacLean, Nancy. *Behind the Mask of Chivalry: The Making of the Second Ku Klux Klan*. New York: Oxford University Press, 1994.

Mappen, Marc. *Jerseyana: The Underside of New Jersey History*. New Brunswick, NJ: Rutgers University Press, 1994.

———. *Prohibition Gangsters: The Rise and Fall of a Bad Generation*. New Brunswick, NJ: Rutgers University Press, 2013.

Mappen, Marc, and Gary Saretzky. *Prohibition in New Jersey: The Bootlegger Era*. Manalapan, NJ: Monmouth County Archives, 2013.

Pine, Alan S., Jean C. Hershenov and Aaron H. Lefkowitz. *Peddler to Suburbanite: The History of the Jews of Monmouth County from the Colonial Period to 1980*. Freehold, NJ: Monmouth Jewish Community Council, 1981.

Regan, Brian. *Gothic Pride: The Story of Building a Great Cathedral in Newark*. New Brunswick, NJ: Rivergate Press, 2012.

Sanger, Margaret. *The Autobiography of Margaret Sanger*. Mineola, NY: Dover Publications, 2017. First published 1938 by W.W. Norton and Company (New York).

Tomlinson, Gerald. *Fatal Tryst*. Lake Hopatcong, NJ: Home Run Press, 1999.

Wade, Wyn Craig. *The Fiery Cross: The Ku Klux Klan in America*. New York: Oxford University Press, 1987.

Wolff, Daniel. *4th of July, Asbury Park: A History of the Promised Land*. New York: Bloomsbury USA, 2008

Zimmer, Kenyon. *Immigrants Against the State: Jewish and Italian Anarchism in America*. Urbana: University of Illinois Press, 2015.

Articles

Coleman, John A. "Religious Liberty." *America* (November 28, 2005).

Furer, Howard B. "The Perth Amboy Riots of 1923." *New Jersey History* 87 (1969).

Kuntz, Jerry. "George H. Lawson: The Rogue Who Tried to Reform Baseball." *The Baseball Research Journal* 37 (2008).

Murray, Aife. "The Ku Klux Klan at Home in Hillsdale." *New Jersey Studies: An Interdisciplinary Journal* (Summer 2017).

Pegram, Thomas R. "Hoodwinked: The Ku Klux Klan and the Anti-Saloon League in 1920s Prohibition Enforcement." *The Journal of the Gilded Age and Progressive Era* 7, no. 1 (January 2008).

Rothman, Joshua. "When Bigotry Paraded Through the Streets." *The Atlantic* (December 4, 2016).

Troppoli, Donna. "The Invisible Boardwalk Empire: The Ku Klux Klan in Monmouth County During the 1920s." *Garden State Legacy*, no. 28 (June 2015).

Manuscripts

Luzky, Colonel (Ret.) Len. "History, 1st Battalion, 372nd Infantry (Rifle) New Jersey National Guard." Unpublished lineage document. NGMMNJ Collection.

Archival Sources

Bernard Bush Collection, Alexander Library. Rutgers University: New Brunswick, NJ.

George H. Moss Jr. Historical Collection of Stereo Views and Ephemera, Guggenheim Memorial Library. Monmouth University: West Long Branch, NJ.

InfoAge Museum. Wall Township, NJ.

JOUAM Fellowship Forum 1926. Bush Collection, Rutgers University Library: New Brunswick, NJ.

Monmouth County Archives, Monmouth County Library. Manalapan, NJ.

Monmouth County Clerk's Office: Freehold, NJ.

Newspapers and Periodicals

Asbury Park Press

Bernardsville (NJ) *News*

Bridgewater (NJ) *Courier News*

Chatham (NJ) *Press*

Decatur (IL) *Herald*

Frederick (MD) *Daily News*

Freehold *Transcript*

Issues of Today (NY)
Keyport (NJ) *Weekly*
Louisville (KY) *Courier Journal*
Marshall (TX) *News Messenger*
Minneapolis Star
Monmouth Inquirer
Newark (NJ) *Evening News*
Newark (NJ) *Ledger*
New Brunswick (NJ) *Home News*
New York Times
Ocean Grove Times
The Oshkosh (WI)
Philadelphia Inquirer
Red Bank Register
San Bernardino County Sun
Time
Trenton Times
Vineland (NJ) *Daily Journal*

Other Sources

Oklahoma Commission. *Tulsa Race Riot: A Report by the Oklahoma Commission to Study the Tulsa Race Riot of 1921*. Tulsa, February 2001.

INDEX

ABOUT THE AUTHORS

Joseph G. Bilby received his BA and MA degrees in history from Seton Hall University and served as a lieutenant in the First Infantry Division in Vietnam in 1966–67. He is assistant curator of the New Jersey National Guard and Militia Museum in Sea Girt, a columnist for the *Civil War News* and *New Jersey Sportsmen News* and a freelance writer, historian and historical consultant. He is the author, editor or co-author of more than four hundred articles and twenty-two books on New Jersey, the Civil War and firearms history. Mr. Bilby has received the Jane Clayton Award for contributions to Monmouth County, New Jersey history; an award of merit from the New Jersey Historical Commission for his contributions to the state's military history; and the New Jersey Meritorious Service Medal from the state's Division of Military and Veterans Affairs. In 2018, he was awarded the Richard J. Hughes Prize by the New Jersey Historical Commission for his lifelong contributions to New Jersey history.

Harry Ziegler received his BA degree in English from Monmouth University and his M.Ed from Georgian Court University and worked for many years at the *Asbury Park Press*, New Jersey's second largest newspaper. He rose from reporter to bureau chief, editor and managing editor of the paper. He is now associate principal of Saint Thomas Aquinas High School in Edison, New Jersey, and this is the eighth book he has co-authored on New Jersey history.